# Womanhood

## IDENTITY TO INTIMACY AND EVERYTHING IN BETWEEN

A WOMEN'S
EMPOWERMENT
COLLECTIVE

# KRYSTAL CASEY

## ALONG WITH 14 INSPIRING WOMEN AUTHORS

*Foreword by Julia Kirby*

# Table of Contents

# FOREWORD
## By Julia Kirby

Dear Reader,

If you're anything like me, you find relief, reassurance, and guidance from hearing another woman's story. Krystal has collected many stories here that, when pieced together, create an honest picture of what it is to walk through the world as a woman. Sometimes, the journey can become so overwhelming that we don't know where to start. This book is your starting point, your tribe. It is a compilation of issues that we deal with but don't really talk about.

Through her life experience, writing, speaking, and coaching, Krystal is more than equipped to crack open these kinds of conversations safely, with expert consideration. I am grateful for the time, effort, and passion she has dedicated towards putting these voices on paper and offering an abundance of empathy and wisdom through her work. I am a young widow and mother myself and have a shared belief in the importance of finding what is good beyond dark times. I appreciate and trust her guiding light. *Womanhood* provides us with a place to sit together and acknowledge each other's brave and bold attempts at life, love, and healing, especially when you feel there are no obvious rules or solutions.

During the worst times in my life, the best women around me have shown up. There's something inside women that fundamentally understands community and the importance of coming together in hard times. They say it takes a village and when I was thirty-one and my husband died just days after the birth of my son, I sure let it. I watched how they instinctively held my newborn baby, fed me, and cared for me. How bittersweet, the way our broken hearts and confused minds can bring us closer to the women around us when we step into vulnerability.

Women know what's up.

In life, there's no getting away from times of fear, loneliness, and confusion. That is when you lean on the women and stories like the ones in this book.

The unpredictable path of womanhood is full of love and loss, and then always more love again. I encourage you to turn to the resources and support inside this book as you write your own chapters. Please, share these stories as well as your own with the women you know, and keep the conversations flowing around all the taboos we deal with as women. In *Womanhood* the authors remind us that we are all human and that at whatever age or stage, there is nothing wrong with us. They understand the value of sharing what others might feel is easier left unspoken. We are encouraged to walk our weird and wacky womanly paths with pride.

I hope you curl up with this book and let Krystal's brave mission and the support from these women wrap you up in love and hope and serve as your go-to guide for discovering, or re-discovering, your voice, vision, and passion in this lifetime. Your heart is beating, so keep searching for ways to stretch it, soothe it, and soar.

Julia
Founder of Widow's Fire
www.widowsfire.com

# INTRODUCTION

How did you come to understand what it means to be a woman? Did you watch your mom as she navigated life's trials, or did you forge your own unique path into womanhood? For some of us, the lessons came by way of witnessing our mother's battle with addiction, enduring the pain of abuse, or carrying the heavy burden of unhealed wounds. For others, it was growing up without our mothers, left to unravel the intricacies of womanhood alone. Yet, we all share a common thread: an unwavering determination to find our way.

In the intricate tapestry of womanhood, there are threads of experiences, challenges, and triumphs that weave together to form the essence of who we are. *Womanhood: Identity to Intimacy and Everything in Between* is not just a book; it is a guide, a haven, and a celebration of the diverse paths that women walk.

After becoming a widow at the age of 35, I found myself contemplating the conversations I haven't had yet with my four young daughters. I thought about all of those difficult, yet essential, discussions about womanhood, intimacy, and sexuality that are often shrouded in silence and shame. I reflected on the ways that the definition of womanhood has changed over the years. It was then that the idea for this book took root—a book that would be more than just words on pages, but a lifeline for those seeking comfort, understanding, and empowerment.

In the pages that follow, we embark on a transformative journey, fearlessly exploring some of the taboo and deeply personal aspects of being a woman. We shed light on these unspoken topics and shatter the barriers that have silenced our voices for far too long. Each chapter is a window into the lives of remarkable women who have generously shared their stories of resilience, vulnerability, and growth.

This book is more than just a collection of stories; it is a reference point and a manual for women who may not have had anyone to talk to about the sensitive issues presented here. We want this book to become a treasured resource—one that you'll keep close, refer back to, and pass along to all the women in your life, empowering them and empowering future generations.

As we dive into themes like embracing your identity, building healthy connections, and talking about the hard things, we invite you to approach each page with an open heart and mind. Let this book be a reminder that you are not alone, that your experiences matter, and that your voice is essential in redefining the narrative of womanhood.

I extend my deepest gratitude to all of the courageous women who have shared their stories and wisdom within these pages. Your bravery and vulnerability have illuminated a path for others to find their voices and walk this journey with resilience and pride.

Together, we are creating a world where womanhood knows no bounds, where authentic conversations bloom, and where empowerment becomes the guiding light for every woman, girl, and future generation.

Welcome to *Womanhood*. May this book be a source of inspiration, comfort, and validation, igniting a spark within you to embrace your authentic self and find strength in the collective sisterhood of women.

# PART 1:
## Embracing Your Identity

From the very beginning, my journey through womanhood has been filled with challenges and uncertainties. Raised primarily by my father and the women in his circle, I often found myself longing for a safe, female presence to guide me through the complexities of becoming a woman.

As I reached different milestones like getting my period, talking to boys, or learning to shave, I yearned for someone who could offer understanding and support (instead of a lecture or a trip to the drugstore).

Here we're diving deep into the heart of womanhood, exploring those intimate and sometimes taboo subjects we might not have had the chance to discuss openly. From the emotional impact of growing up without a mother figure to the empowering process of discovering and embracing our authentic selves, we're here to share our stories and offer understanding.

## Stephanie Brandolini

Founder of Brandolini Ink

Writing Portfolio Site: stephbrandolini.wixsite.com/portfolio
Copywriting & Creative Coaching Business Site:
stephbrandolini.wixsite.com/brandolini-ink
www.linkedin.com/in/stephaniebrandolini/
www.facebook.com/sbrandolini
www.instagram.com/stephbrandolini/

Stephanie Brandolini, award-winning screenwriter, author and novelist, channels trauma and psychic insight into transformative tales of resilience. An architect of otherworldly realms grounded in the human experience, her psychologically inclined science fantasy narratives transform pain into empowerment, speaking to the universal journey of overcoming adversity. Drawing from her phoenix-like rise from personal mental health struggles, Stephanie creates characters that vanquish their demons—mirroring her own path of healing and self-discovery.

As an intuitive copywriter, ghostwriter and creative coach, Stephanie leverages her unique abilities to help spiritual entrepreneurs elevate their businesses, crafting not just compelling sales stories, but building bridges to her client's personal growth.

Stephanie's work is a testament to rebirth, illuminating the path for others with her evocative storytelling.

# TRANSFORMING YOUR DEEPEST WOUNDS INTO FUEL FOR YOUR CALLING

By Stephanie Brandolini

What whispers to you from your soul's depths?
What urges you forth when you have nothing left?
What passion calls loudest to be expressed?

That, my friend, is your calling.

Can you allow yourself to hear it?
Can you allow yourself to feel it?
Can you allow your calling to guide you into going for it?

Throughout this chapter I'll share my story of heeding my calling—and I mean all of it: the good, bad, and the ugly—intended to catalyze an inner awakening that I hope will allow you to open to the wonder of your own calling.

## What Lies Beneath?

As women, who are we?

For centuries we've been suppressed, dishonored, devalued, persecuted—and unfortunately, in many parts of the world, this is still common practice.

We may ask, how did it come to this? We may even look for someone to blame, and often our common scapegoat is, you guessed it, the Patriarchy.

While the ideology of the Patriarchy is still enforced in way too many countries and brings injustice to all genders, times have changed enough for so many women worldwide to reclaim their voices, power, and sovereignty.

This is not solely a time for women to rise, it's an opportunity for the collective of the human race to ascend in consciousness.

Through this collaborative feminist reclamation, it's my hope that we can come to a place where the divine feminine and masculine in all of us can rise and work together towards a middle ground of equanimity, reciprocity, and harmony for the world.

But there's a problem many can't see because it's beneath the surface—untreated wounds that have festered in their neglect.

There are matrices of generational trauma and past life wounds we get to heal and break free from in this lifetime. Not to mention the ones we've accumulated in our current lives.

These wounds are buried so deep we often don't even realize we have them, yet they dictate our fear-based reactions to the modern world. They compound upon each other like knots in our individual and collective tapestries, winding tighter and tighter until we're confined in warped ways of thinking we can no longer see our way out of.

But what if—as a united collective—we took a look beneath our surfaces, delved into the abyss, and pulled on that string that would unravel it all?

## Reclaiming My Calling

Ever since I can remember, I've been in love with stories. I taught myself to read around the age of five. My mum would find me sounding out words I'd never been taught to read, transfixed on how they evoked images and meaning within me. She'd ask me, "How do you know what it says?" My answer?

"I just know."

As children we have this innate sense of knowing our highest level. This self-belief gets lost along the way as we grapple with the expectations of society, family, friends, and our unrealistically high expectations of ourselves. The latter was especially true for me as I fell into the traps of perfectionism and people-pleasing—to name a few. Through cycles of becoming enmeshed in expectations and trauma-led fear responses, I had become a self I didn't even recognize.

Child Me knew storytelling was her calling, but as I grew up enduring bullying, family discord, and a severe eating disorder—alongside all the shame, anxiety, and depression the disorder entailed—self-belief became a lost notion I could no longer even fathom as an adult.

There's an evil stigma in our culture that creative work is "just a hobby," that "you can't make money with it," and worst of all in my case, the concept of the "starving artist."

I took those untrue notions way too seriously and ended up in jobs I didn't really want for, you guessed it, the money. All the while neglecting my true ambition.

It took me many years of going the wrong way before I could get back to the childhood belief in myself I once had from an empowered place of confidence, possibility, and trust.

Despite the challenges on my journey thus far—and honestly, even inspired by them—it was worth every tear, heartbreak, and moment of suffering to reclaim my calling and GO FOR IT!

## From Figuring It Out to Feeling It Out

My journey into going for it as a storytelling entrepreneur began, as all stories do, with a catalyst. An incident that spurred me into action to finally let go and follow my dreams.

We experience countless catalysts in life—some we heed and some we run away from.

Then there are the pivotal catalysts—the ones that get you up off the proverbial bathroom floor and seek the tools to change your reality.

A pivotal catalyst struck me in a moment when I became aware enough to recognize that I was stuck in self-destructive patterns of substance abuse and attracting men who didn't truly value me.

And let me tell you, that hit all the nails in the coffin at once.

To top that off, I further realized the eating disorder I thought I'd overcome still reared its seductive, nasty head in moments of high stress—a coping mechanism running like an outdated program within me.

My familiar friend at the time, Despair, beckoned me to her dark depths. Oh, how the urge to sink into her, to not see what I just saw, and put the blinders back on tempted me.

But in that moment I *knew* I couldn't. There was no going back once I saw the mess of myself clearly. The option was to devolve or...

## Evolve

At this point, I was in my early 30s and a big part of me thought that I was "too old" to start over. I can laugh at this absurdity now; it's a common plague that's infected every gender, but it's women and those who identify as such, who are affected most profoundly. That dreaded "biological clock" that's supposedly ticking us into doom is like an albatross around our necks holding us in patterns, relationships, jobs, and situations that don't fucking serve us!

Why?

Now that's a good question. Security comes to mind here. The security of the system society has put in place for us...

Well, I don't know about you, but to me, that's limiting as fuck and

I'm sick of seeing so many talented, powerful, magickal women sucked into it.

But how do we get out of it?

## Your Transformational Keys

There are many keys you'll discover as you embark on your transformational path to your calling, each acting as a signal from the Universe that you're on the right path. Some will slide into locks seamlessly, others will feel rusty—jarring—and you'll likely want to keep that door shut.

But as you forge ahead, your calling gets louder and stronger until it's like a beacon pulling you forth. So even though parts of you won't want to go any further—will want to give up and settle—your higher self within, pulling you to where you need to go without, won't be able to help it.

The most valuable Transformational Key I've reclaimed is my intuition. Remember Child Me who knew her calling from the get-go? She had intuition in spades and didn't even know what it was yet!

Intuition can be defined as a natural, subconscious, and instinctive ability to understand or perceive something without the need for conscious reasoning or evidence. It's a deep inner knowing that arises spontaneously—but can be honed and called upon at will—providing insights, guidance, and understanding beyond logical or rational thinking.

It was the "beyond logical or rational thinking" part that stumped me for so long. You see, as creative as I am, I'm equally analytical, and that logically oriented, hyper-independent masculine side of myself was exaggerated due to my father wound.

Father wounds run deep, especially for women as we tend to pattern our choices in lovers and partners after them. This was a fact I refused to see for so long which only exacerbated the wound, causing it to fester and become more of a monster than it really was.

I resisted being a girl with daddy issues. The result?

I created more issues than were ever really there in the first place. Like the mythical Gorgon Hercules fought, when I resisted one head another would emerge.

I've come to a place now where I know that my dad was a good man who truly did the best he could. A great reader and a writer himself with the gift of poetic prose. He dreamed of a songwriting career, but alcoholism stood in his way. This was a block he went to his grave with, dream unrealized.

My dad's addiction to alcohol caused so much strife between my parents that Child Me felt caught in the crossfire, along with my younger brother. To make a game of it we would eavesdrop on them. I had a morbid fascination with their fighting that I don't know I'll ever fully understand, but when it comes to healing these wounds sometimes you're not meant to know all the whys and reasoning behind them; you're meant to face them, feel them, and let them go.

As much as I loved my dad, it terrified me to think of falling prey to addiction like him. This became another form of resistance that was a huge contributor to my similar addiction block of an eating disorder.

My dream of becoming a storytelling entrepreneur saved me from my block, and a part of me judged my dad for not having the capability to do this himself. However, by following my intuition to spiritual and energetic healing practices, I discovered more and more keys to unlock me from the prison I'd made for myself.

These keys are found when we heal our deepest wounds, which can be terrifying to face and will take patience, practice, and repetition to work through the many layers of trauma surrounding them.

Deep wounds have often festered over time from repeated patterns of suppression and avoidance. And seriously, who wants to face a festering wound? No one! But would you rather let them worsen and live the rest of your life operating from the fear, pain, and trauma these wounds are inducing, or will you choose to listen to that inner guidance that brought you to these pages?

I guarantee you're reading this for a reason—and that reason is tied to your soul's calling. It's that calling you have locked in your heart of hearts that will fuel you to keep going.

My deepest wound that I had to face many times over was the memory of my mum and dad's worst fight over my dad's drinking which resulted in my dad hitting my mum.

This had never happened before. My dad was a lover, not a fighter, but the addiction had so much of a hold on him that he lashed out in a moment that broke our family apart for good. My mum was forced to call the police to intervene, and I couldn't help but watch the disastrous scene unfold as I saw my dad arrested and my mum visibly wounded in the process. My mum then needed my help to take pictures of her in her bruised-up state for evidence.

I'd already created so many stories around my parent's fighting, all of them misinterpreted around me thinking that I was somehow at fault or the cause of their conflict. Was I a burden that caused my dad to drink? Was I unwanted? Was I unloved?

As much as storytelling is my dream and passion, it has a dark side in the negative narratives I'd spin for myself out of fear, worry, and uncertainty.

This wound from my parent's worst fight added another layer to my misinterpreting, overthinking mind. I misconstrued from this explosive fight that this was how marriages went; that if, as a woman, you tried to help the man you loved out of harmful habits, you were bothering him, and if you asked for what you wanted, you only got a fight out of it.

It took me years of deep diving back into this wound and many others that I'd extrapolated from it to realize all of this. Energetic Neuro Linguistic Programming (ENLP), Cognitive Behavioral Therapy (CBT), Intuitive Energy Healing, Meditation, Sound Therapy, Priestess Training… I've tried it all and then some. All worked in their own ways for me, but because I'd rebuilt my foundation through an Intuition Training Program with a Priestess Path Mentor—who became a beloved writing client—I was able to absorb what worked for me and release what didn't.

One of those keys unlocked my power of forgiveness. This allowed me to accept my dad, myself, and the wealth of my experience with him that, in its own way, healed me by being an example of what not to do.

My spiritual relationship with my dad is now one of my greatest sources of empowerment since his passing in the summer of 2019. I know that my soul chose him to be my father to teach, hone, and inspire me to become the writer I am today.

That's not to say I don't miss him. Don't ache to physically hug him and tell him all that's in my heart. But I know he knows, and he's in a greater place beyond this where he's at peace and held in the love of the divine.

I don't just know it—I *know* it on a soul level. For me, this intuitive knowing resonates like a shiver through my heart that tells me I'm on the right path. Different people feel these intuitive nudges in the body in different places. For many it's a "gut instinct," telling you yes or no to people, situations, and choices that arise on your path. I invite you to feel into where you feel these nudges, and next time you're unsure of what to do, who to trust, or where to go… let it guide you. It might not make logical sense, but it will feel right. It's under that right feeling that your innate knowing lies, powering the feeling to propel you forward.

Following your intuition can feel scary at first; after all, you're stretching into something new and, to your ego, that's a definite no-go. It's tapping into a deeper level of wisdom, accessing information that's beyond the scope of the conscious mind. It's also not a one-and-done kind of thing; it's a lifelong, unfolding journey into unknown possibilities that reveals your truth, power, and calling along the way.

Following my intuition led me to serve with my writing. I started by building my portfolio of TV pilots and film screenplays that have since won numerous awards. Then I branched out into books and copywriting which planted the seed for me to start my company, Brandolini Ink, where I support a diverse range of consciously-led entrepreneurs, writers, and creatives with my writing services.

Listening to my calling and unlocking my true potential has allowed me to thrive and grow, both as a person and professionally. I hope my story has sparked a seed for you to do the same in your own way.

Remember, it's a lifelong journey, and support is in abundance. To start or enhance your journey with consciously-driven writing and creativity, explore my websites, sign up for my newsletter, or schedule a free consultation. I'd love to connect with you and help you create something extraordinary!

## Becky Vale

Writer

Why is she not a jailbird like her mother or a bitter drunk like her older sister? Meet Becky Vale, your guide to unconventional success, like mastering 'quid pro quo' at work or faking pregnancies – just kidding!

Join Becky on her journey through life's uncertainties and insecurities. With two decades as a health educator and former Aurora University adjunct professor, she's an expert at crafting curriculums and community resource fairs. She also co-founded the DeKalb SHARE Chapter, supporting families dealing with infant/pregnancy loss.

Becky is a sought-after writer, delving into motherhood's complexities in Fell's 5-Star series "Grief Diaries." As a female soldier, she confronted misogyny during Operation Enduring Freedom/Operation Iraqi Freedom. Additionally, she's inspired, humored, and encouraged readers as a Daily Chronicle columnist of "The Sex Professor" and "Cheeky Mama."

Learn from Becky the power of knowledge and vulnerability on your path to becoming a thriving woman.

# NO MOTHER? NO PROBLEM

By Becky Vale

## A Rotten Childhood

Picture this: little two-year-old me huddled under the kitchen table, my trusty doggie by my side furiously lapping away my tears as I await my mama's return. Finally, the sound of her car pulling up sends me crawling to the door in a flash. With a gleeful grin, Mama holds up a bag of pancakes. She looks at me, puzzled, and asks, "Why's she crying? Why's she making Mama feel bad? After all, she was the hungry one, not Mama."

So there I am, little Becky, wiping away my boogers to gobble down those pancakes until my hunger pangs surrender, then generously offering the rest to my ever-loyal doggie under the table. Yep, even at that tender age I knew something wasn't quite right with this woman.

## Barbara's Troubles - WTH Mom?

Barbara, my mom, had a knack for turning bad situations into something even worse. Her questionable judgment often landed us in hot water, especially when it came to her tumultuous love life. I can't unsee those cringe-worthy moments on the couch—yikes. One time, a guy even spat on me for crying about it. These toxic relationships usually culminated in the police being called, either for her hitting or stalking these poor guys. Some nights, she'd end up in jail and the battery convictions just kept piling up.

Now Barbara, bless her heart, pointed the finger at her ex-husband for our life in the poverty lane. But let's face it: her frequent job losses and lack of education were the real culprits, leading to a laundry list of criminal activities and bouts of homelessness. Barb had a peculiar talent for writing bad checks repeatedly. One of her less-than-stellar boyfriends even introduced her to the world of money laundering, and many of those escapades ended in fraudulent convictions. My mom got slapped with probation, but she had a knack for breaking it. That led to stints in work release programs, but she inevitably lost those jobs too. It was a never-ending cycle that resulted in her not showing up for her work release.

And that's how Barb found herself with a warrant for her arrest. The cops showed up at our door when I was about sixteen. My mother insisted I lie to the cops, and being the dutiful daughter I was, I did. She then demanded a ride to her boyfriend's house which, of course, ended in a traffic stop and both of us in handcuffs. I was slapped with an obstructing justice charge and probation. Meanwhile, my mother was transferred to the hospital for a gallbladder attack which ultimately caused her own demise. Barb, true to form, decided to make a break for it. An officer pursued her into the hospital parking lot, and that's when things went from crazy to full-on insane. My mom started playing hide-and-seek between cars, pretending she had a gun in her pocket. Eventually, the cop nabbed her, and Barb was charged with a laundry list of felonies including resisting arrest, endangering a cop, breaking probation, and more. She ended up serving five years in a maximum-security prison for being a flight risk and putting an officer in danger.

Absolutely bonkers, right? I mean, what the hell Barb?

Let me make one thing clear—Barbara is not your run-of-the-mill woman. My mother wrestles with a mental illness that impairs her ability to hold down a job, maintain relationships, and even take care of herself physically. Empathy? Well, that's not exactly in her skill set when it comes to my sister and me. Barbara never took any accountability for her actions; instead, she manipulated my sister and me, often pitting us against each other. She intentionally tore our family apart. Again, seriously, what the hell Barb?

As if that wasn't enough, my mother couldn't even teach me the basics of hygiene. To this day, she's more of a sporadic shower-taker, subsists on a diet that would make a health nut cringe, couldn't be bothered with a bra, and almost always has grime under her nails. And, if you can believe it, she occasionally just lets it all go in her pants. I mean, what in the ever-loving hell Barbara?

Growing up without a role model seriously messed with my head. I can assure you that I had no aspirations of becoming a jailbird or someone who couldn't keep their pants clean.

So, what's a girl to do, right?

Well, I made bank by becoming a drug-smuggling mastermind from Peru—haha, just kidding! Seriously though, I went from trashy to classy the old-fashioned way: by sleeping with my bosses! Haha, kidding again.

What I genuinely aspired to be was happy. And, dear reader, I'm here to tell you that I found happiness, and I hope my journey can help you find it too.

## Finding Resilience

At seventeen, I moved in with my best friend, Annabelle. Her parents graciously took me under their wing because, well, my mother was in that maximum-security prison. I didn't take their support for granted. My boyfriend Max's parents even lent me a car so I could work. They helped me find my stride. I'll forever be grateful to them, and it's a big reason why I now give back to my family and friends.

I realized that the future was in my hands, so I graduated early from high school and enlisted in the Army. Boot camp? Holy crap, it was a nightmare. But I powered through, and as a bonus, I got into fantastic shape. I even earned a physical fitness medal - a testament to my newfound resolve.

The National Guard also opened the doors to education. During this time, I started seeing a counselor who helped me confront the trauma I had endured during my tumultuous upbringing. Unpacking those experiences wasn't easy, and I often found myself in tears. The counselor diagnosed me with childhood trauma, a revelation that both shocked and liberated me. It was as though a light had been shone on the darkness of my past, and I could finally begin the healing process.

With hard work, I graduated with a degree in education. Then I landed a fantastic teaching position without any bedroom favors involved. I was thrilled to have a job with full benefits, a far cry from the instability I had known growing up. The first thing I did was fix my front tooth, a symbol of my newfound self-reliance.

At this point, my life was undeniably better, but I wasn't truly happy. I had survived but I wanted more—I wanted to thrive. It was then that a doctor prescribed an antidepressant that changed my perspective on life. I suddenly had the energy and clarity to move beyond mere survival and start embracing the joy of living. For the first time, I felt a genuine passion for life and an undeniable yearning to thrive.

A friend introduced me to the concept of a gratitude journal. After exploring many stress management skills, this simple practice had a profound impact on my outlook on life. Each morning, I'd start my day by stretching, sipping coffee, and journaling about the things I was grateful for. On the toughest days, I'd journal again at night. It became my sanctuary, a space where I could express love for the positive things in my life. Practicing this brings comfort during challenging times.

## Crafting a Vision of Happiness

My therapist also encouraged me to create a vision board. I bought a large white poster board and flipped through magazines, cutting out images of the things I hoped to achieve in life. It was a revelation for me—realizing my dreams were attainable and worth pursuing. As I created my vision board, I realized that while I wanted a family in the future, there was so much more I wanted to experience and accomplish before settling down. My heart wanted to travel, sing, and grow! I had a thirst for life and adventure that couldn't be quenched by domesticity alone.

Now, let's be honest, not everything on my vision board has come to fruition. Some goals I've neglected, others I've outgrown. But the act of creating these boards, or as I like to call them "slide decks", has become a personal ritual. Allowing yourself to dream makes you feel empowered. Please know happiness is subjective. Happiness can be the classic all-American dream or not. Give yourself the opportunity to become whatever your heart desires.

Vision boards help you plan personal experiences only you can fulfill. For instance, being a karaoke queen is not a priority for a lot of people. But I found my over-the-top performance to be a release for me and entertainment for others. My visions have allowed me to travel the world. I have seen the most beautiful places and handsome faces. My tears dripped in Pompeii and I swam with the wild dolphins in Australia.

As an educator, I have a knack for storytelling. I had an eagerness to write. I took a chance on a topic and met with the local newspaper editor. That's how my days as "Cheeky Mama" were born. This first column was a platform that gave me laughs but, more importantly, it gave me a connection to a community. Corresponding with my readers felt like I was putting down roots in my dear farm town, something I never had as a kid but was creating for myself as an adult —and my soon-to-be family. Now, here I am, writing another book, trying to provide connection and advice, because I would've loved that for myself earlier on.

To this day, Barb tries to rear her ugly head. She has realized that I have been enjoying my life. She also realized I was earning money. Barb started asking me to buy her stuff. She nearly demanded I buy her a car. For my own protection, I decided to create more defined boundaries. As my joy continued into marriage and the birth of my daughter, the boundaries became high-privacy gates. I refused to let Barb take my adulthood away from me too.

My love and energy were guarded for my husband, my doggies, and most importantly my daughter, Heather.

Heather deserves all the enjoyment life has to offer. Every day, I try to model healthy behaviors. She has picked up the habit of journaling while sipping juice, not coffee. On Sundays, we plan school outfits, charge her Chromebook, double-check her homework, and get her water bottles ready for softball practice. I know developing these simple habits will help ease the days to make more space for fun.

Though, already, navigating friendships is challenging. I tell Heather not to compare herself with others or judge them either. Be who you want to be. I think it is rubbing off as Heather is up for taking chances. When she dances, the whole room dances. Her eagerness to learn new sports or crafts is a testament to her confidence. I know the attitude she throws at me is the start of independence. Hopefully, it is a growing sense of advocacy as well. Heather shares her ups and downs with me. Those tender moments of tears and laughter are cherished. I am not a perfect mom but I am a happy mom. Throughout the years, I will try to guide Heather to follow her heart. I will teach her that grit, education, and self-love will lead her to happiness. Who knows? One day, she may stop thinking my vision boards are stupid.

My journey from a rotten childhood to a life filled with love and possibility wasn't without its hardships. Looking back it's evident that I could have made much more money smuggling drugs! Haha - Just kidding! I settled for using my wit and grit to go from a girl who accomplished so much to a woman who still does. But if my story can inspire even one person to believe in the power of transformation, then it's a story worth sharing.

So, dear reader, whether you're navigating your own challenges or seeking inspiration to chart a new path in life, know that you are not alone. I've been there, and I've come out the other side stronger and happier than I ever thought possible. You can, too. I hope that my story will serve as a guiding light, a reminder that resilience and determination can lead to a life filled with joy, purpose, and boundless opportunities.

## Stephanie Taylor

Founder of Styled by Stephanie

www.styledbystephaniellc.com
www.linkedin.com/in/stephanie-taylor-4582a093
www.facebook.com/YourStylistStyledbyStephanieLLC
www.instagram.com/styledbystephaniellc/

Stephanie, owner of Styled by Stephanie, believes in the power of curated brand identity to empower your true authentic self to shine brightly. Stephanie is a business mentor, public speaker, author, stylist, and brand campaign organizer. She is dedicated to helping you craft a brand that authentically represents your passion, keeps you motivated to chase your dreams, and connects you to like-minded people.

Through engaging public speaking events and her transformative mentoring approach, Stephanie motivates entrepreneurs to uncover their unique essence and showcase it through their brand. By fostering connections among small businesses, she creates a supportive community where collaboration thrives.

With Stephanie's guidance, your brand will radiate authenticity and passion, leaving a lasting impact on your audience. Let Stephanie be your trusted partner in curating a brand identity that elevates your business and allows your true authentic self to shine through. Let's make your dreams a reality.

# LET ME INTRODUCE YOU TO, YOU

By Stephanie Taylor

It was a beautifully cozy, brisk, and sunny fall afternoon in Green Bay, Wisconsin; Mother Nature was preparing us for the cold winter to come. I woke up early with a burst of inspiration and ready to tackle my day. I had been planning a mini-shopping adventure all week. I may have even been a little over-prepared by going on Pinterest to find looks and styles I loved. I ended up creating four different lookboards for inspiration. My main focus was finding a few new, fun, colorful pieces for a vacation I was taking to the Greek Islands, along with a few new pieces for my work wardrobe. I wanted to feel fresh and beautiful. After all, this was my first vacation in over five years and I had recently lost 25 pounds!

I stood in the dressing room of a lovely local boutique, staring at my reflection in a tall, full-length mirror. About to cry, I thought to myself:

"I don't understand; nothing is fitting me right."

"I didn't even eat before I came here today, I know I'm not bloated."

"I came prepared and nothing is what I envisioned."

"I do not feel beautiful."

"Nothing looks good on me."

"I know this woman, Seraphina, who shops here all the time and has this shirt. She always looks so cute and we are about the same size."

"What is wrong with me?"

"I just need to lose a little more weight here and there. Then I know this will look good on me."

"I'll buy this piece for when I get down to my goal weight."

That day I left my favorite boutique feeling defeated and so discouraged, far from fresh and beautiful. My mindset and self-limiting beliefs had me fooled, thinking I was the problem.

"If only ___ was different about me."

Please don't tell me I'm the only one who has had these false conversations with themself full of self-limiting beliefs! The conversations where we feel we are the problem. We start having a self-destructive inner dialogue. As if we have to fit into a pre-written guideline of beauty standards that are already set for us.

Who sets those standards? Designers? Media? Magazines? Hollywood? The Internet? Keep in mind, beauty standards are constantly evolving and changing; it's hard to "Keep up with the Jones". Starting from The Golden Era of Hollywood, 1930s-1950s, where curves were considered beautiful - hourglass figure, large breasts, and a slim waist. Leading to the Vibrant 60s where being willowy was considered beautiful - thin with longer arms and legs, with more of a lean youthful build. Skipping a few eras brings us to The Heroin Chic Era, the 1990s, where being pale and underweight was beautiful - translucent skin, exceedingly thin, and an androgynous appeal. Standards change so much that it's ever-evolving. More and more, we fail to appreciate ourselves in all the aspects we strive for in fear of being judged or not truly understanding ourselves.

Have you ever been shopping and seen something that you absolutely loved, but passed it up? Maybe it wasn't what the fashion standards were at the time. Were you shy or scared about what your friends and family might think, or maybe your peers and colleagues?

It's daunting, almost exhausting, to imagine what other people's opinions are and to keep up with what society tells us is acceptable.

This is a perfect recipe to create insecurities and really dim your shine. Your environment can make it so easy to lose sight of your own likes and dislikes. Almost as if others know you better than you know yourself, convincing you of what you should think and feel.

It's now your time to take your power back through self-awareness. Get to know yourself and listen to what your soul desires. It gets so easy to block out our own intuition with those fears or judgments of others rolling around in our heads. We feel obligated, in a way, to mold ourselves into what we were raised to believe is acceptable. Know your truth and stand firm in it. Let's start with beauty standards. If I were to ask you, "What do beauty standards mean to you?", would you have an answer?

If you were to ask Google to define beauty standards it would say: "Beauty standards are a set of values applied to the appearance of both men and women to be regarded as beautiful and handsome in order to rightly fit in a community."

That alone is headache-worthy. All the different communities throughout the world have wildly different standards and, as previously discussed, those standards in each era of those communities are constantly changing as well. All my brain got out of that headache is that fashion can be whatever you want it to be - fashion is universal, make it your own. It's an art and you are the canvas.

## Pioneering Your Own Standards

How do you truly get to understand your authentic self, you might ask? There is no simple answer. It's all about getting to know yourself and trusting your intuition. Introducing/re-introducing yourself to aspects of you that you didn't even know existed or remember having. Understanding what motivates you and what story you want to tell the world through the knowledge you gain. What are you trying to accomplish? How does it make you feel?

## Cultivating a New Mindset

It starts with reprogramming our mindsets. One curious thought can lead to a whole new perspective and provide us the urge to take a step back to really listen to one's own intuition. Trust that intuition and let go of fear.

When you are open to learning lessons and open to the signs all around you, it will lead you to the best version of yourself. The possibilities in the word, curiosity, are ones that can be regularly overlooked by doubt. Doubts' roots come from various sources such as fear, traumas, external influences, and low self-esteem, to name a few.

Start by paying attention to the way you talk to yourself. Are you being loving? Nurturing? Or, are you being hard on yourself? Self-doubting?

Once you start becoming aware of how you speak to yourself, then you're able to start rewording the way you speak to yourself. "I can't do that." Why can't you do that? Who told you that you couldn't do that? What self-limiting belief is holding you back? Being aware is powerful.

Let go of the self-limiting beliefs and learn self-love. Speak with good intentions: "I can do that" or "I will do that." Pay attention to how situations make you feel. Why do you feel this way? What is the root of what is bothering you? That is really when your Authentic Self will SHINE the brightest.

Let's be honest though, that is all a lot easier said than done and a lot more work than most of us realize. Just start. Start small; start with one curious thought and see where that curiosity takes you. The power of our thoughts is often underestimated or overlooked. The thoughts we believe are the ones that become our realities. Hold tight to the power within yourself and shine as bright as you want. Becoming more comfortable with who you are allows you to express yourself in ways that feel good to you. Patience and taking it one day at a time are important to remember as nothing happens overnight.

## Getting to Know Your Body's Contours

As you learn about your own body, remind yourself of this little helpful tip: never force your body into a piece of clothing. Allow the clothing to fit and flow onto your body. Build your outfits based on your unique shape, and embrace your body.

If you have ever had the thought "Nothing is fitting me right," let's dive into what could be triggering that thought. Beauty standards aside, consider the fact that our bodies are always in a constant state of change and that embracing the change is not always easy.

Has your body shape changed? Honestly, my body today is not the body I had ten years ago, five years ago, or even six months ago. I'm guessing yours isn't either. That's OK!

Maybe you don't know your body shape. That could be your first curious thought and the start of a new, self-discovery journey. Every body shape has had its era of "beauty standards", let me help you discover yours. It will help to have a basic understanding of what each of the five main body types are. You could even fall into more than one category, nothing is black and white.

- **Apple Shape:** Wide torso, broad shoulders, full bust, and waist. Tend to have thinner arms, legs, and hips.

- **Pear Shape (Triangle):** Hips are wider than your shoulders. Tend to have smaller busts.

- **Rectangle Shape:** Shoulders, bust, and hips are all around the same size. Tend to not have a defined waist.

- **Inverted Triangle Shape:** The shoulders are the widest part of your body. Tend to have narrow hips.

- **Hourglass Shape**: Shoulders and hips are similar in size and you have a smaller, more defined waist.

Taking your measurements in four key areas (shoulders, busts, natural waist, and hips) will determine your body shape the easiest. Jot down each of the four measurements and see what body shape your measurements line up with.

1. **Shoulders**: To take the measurement of your shoulders, measure shoulder to shoulder with the widest distance between your shoulders. It typically falls about 1-2 inches underneath your neckline.

2. **Bust**: Stand straight with your arms relaxed down along your side and feet shoulder length apart. When you take the measurement, measure under your arms and around the fullest part of your bust. The tape measure should have a little give and not be tight to your body.

3. **Natural Waist**: Located right above your belly button and right below your rib cage. If you lean to one side, you will find the natural crease of your waist. That is going to be the area of your body you measure around to determine your natural waistline.

4. **Hips**: Stand straight and have your heels touching. Make sure when measuring that it is around the widest part of your hips.

To quickly determine if you have broad shoulders, ask yourself, when you are wearing a shoulder bag/purse does it fall off your shoulder? Or, do the straps of your tank tops fall down? If so, then you most likely do not have broad shoulders. When you are wearing a fitted shirt, does it feel tight or pull when wearing it? If so, then you could have broad shoulders.

Now, let's determine if you have what is considered a longer torso or a short torso. Take both of your hands, make sure your fingers are pressed together, and place one hand on top of the other right underneath your breast line. If the bottom hand covers your belly button, you most likely have a short torso. If the belly button is below your hand with some space to spare, you most likely have a longer torso. Lastly, if the belly button is just touching the bottom of your hand, you most likely have a balanced torso.

## Styles that Harmonize with Your Body Shape.

Knowing these little details about ourselves helps us tremendously when shopping for the right styles and fits that best work with our bodies. How you feel about your body really reflects how you carry yourself.

One thing I want you to remember: *No matter what fit, style, or cut is recommended for your body type, if you put something on and it breaks every beauty standard, but you feel beautiful in it = WEAR IT!!*

Here are a few recommendations for each body shape:

- **Apple shaped** bodies look flattering in flowing materials such as matte Jersey. Matte jersey is light, airy, and a soft material with a more structured look and it helps to conceal weight in areas we don't want to have materials clinging to. The goal is to have your shoulders look wide and to help your body look longer with a lower neckline (think: v-necks, strapless, square, or scoop necklines).

- **Pear shaped** looks tend to draw attention to the upper body, away from the wider hips. This can be accomplished by bright, beautiful colors of different types of patterns on the upper body. Keywords for dresses and skirts are "fit and flare". Fitted around the waist and flared out over the hips. A-line skirts that end right above the knees are a good option. Fabrics to look for will lightly skim your curves (ex: viscose and cotton).

- **Rectangle shaped** body's goal is to define your waistline to break up the rectangle shape. A dark belt is a quick solution to your outfit. Vivid patterns (ex: horizontal stripes) and bulky fabrics (ex: wool, sherpa) add a chunkier feel that can help give your body the feel of different proportions.

- **Inverted shaped** body's main objective is going to be to create balance with the broader shoulders on the upper body and the narrower lower body. You will not want to have bright bold colors or patterns on your upper body. When choosing a nice pair of jeans make sure to avoid the skinny jeans and wear more of a flared or bootcut style jean. Helpful hint: avoid dark washes of jeans and do your best to have your jeans a lighter color than your shirts.

- **Hourglass shaped** bodies are naturally balanced which makes it one of the goals to not dress in a way that draws one's attention to only the upper or lower body. Do not hide your waist; follow your natural shape. Drawing attention to your waist is the main goal of maintaining proportion here. Your body's natural shape looks beautiful in fabrics like silk blends, chiffon, and spandex. They all will show off those curves.

## Celebrate Your Body's Unique Proportions

Not only is knowing the shape of our body important, but understanding that everyone's proportions are different as well is key. Even though you may both be 5ft 3in at 145lbs, it doesn't mean that you can wear each other's looks. One of you may have a longer torso than the other. One of you may have longer legs. Your bust size could vary as well. Whatever the case is, your proportions are not the same as someone else's and in return, the same looks and styles will not necessarily fit you the same. Fabrics, styles, and cuts look completely different on different body types. Our proportions are more than height; it's how everything looks in context.

I challenge you to strip down to your panties and take a good long look at yourself in the mirror. As you are analyzing your body and inspecting your silhouette, find an area of your body that you are proud to have. One part of your body that brings you confidence.

The challenge is to truly embrace how you are feeling in that moment. Fashion is not only about how you look, it's also about how you feel. If you feel confident you will look confident. If you feel awkward you will look awkward.

As you are learning new things about your body, remember how they are making you feel. It helps to fully understand your mind and body to make sense of the best fashion choices for yourself. Once you find an area of your body that makes you feel confident, find a way to accentuate it so that it accommodates your body's shape and proportions.

Love your legs? Let's find some skirts that show off those legs.
Your arms? Let's start wearing more sleeveless tops.
Your back? How about we find you a perfect open-back dress?

No matter what area of the body you love the most, there is a way to flaunt it. Once you learn about your body, the fun can begin as you dive into the different styles, cuts, patterns, and fabrics made for your body!

The more you get to know your body and really understand how things are making you feel, the easier it is to understand and embrace your own message. The process will slowly re-program your way of thinking, allowing you to be more open to hearing what your true desires are.

Excitement will kick in as you gain clarity and understanding of your voice.

Keep in mind that you are your own brand - how do you want to show up? The energy that you will be able to put into higher vibrational thoughts will elevate you in ways you could not fathom. You can redefine beauty and body image to be whatever you want it to mean to you.

Going through my personal journey, I realized the difference we all can make with the right mindset and drive. I took everything that I learned and turned it into my own passion and brand, Styled by Stephanie. I found a way to help support other people's dreams and am learning how incredibly powerful it truly is. It will undoubtedly amaze you what you're capable of with the right outfit and mindset. Like Marilyn Monroe said, "Give a girl the right pair of shoes and she can conquer the world."

You *can* conquer the world. Do not let the outside noise of society cloud your own personal style and confidence. Beauty is in the eye of the beholder, and it is whatever you want it to be; you are a work of art.

## Krysta Cunningham

Owner of Intentionally Art

www.intentionallyart.com
www.linkedin.com/in/krysta-cunningham-27974128a/
www.facebook.com/intentionally.art/
www.instagram.com/intentionallyart/

Krysta's journey as a photographer began early with a unique ability for capturing images. She earned degrees in Graphic Design, Marketing/Advertising, and Photography. After years of honing her artistic talents she made her mark as a skilled graphic artist with a lifelong passion for photography. You are able to experience her unique perspective through her printed photography. Defined not only by her creative pursuits, Krysta holds the role of neurotic mother to two incredible humans. Love and dedication to her children being her ultimate driving force. As a Breast Cancer warrior, she demonstrates unwavering resilience in the face of adversity. An inspiration to many and a testament to her indomitable spirit. Grateful to have embraced writing as a form of expression and given an opportunity to share her experiences. Krysta's personal values, resilience and creativity guide her in life, continuing to inspire her to create a positive impact.

# CELEBRATING DIVERSE EXPERIENCES AND ENCOURAGING INCLUSIVITY

By Krysta Cunningham

Some people believe everyone has three great loves in a lifetime. Others believe in a soulmate. One true love. We are taught from an early age that if you meet someone special you better hold on tight - don't let go. That we are destined to find one other human on this planet and live happily ever after. Ah yes, the happily ever after. Hold that thought. Let's rewind a bit.

For most of my life, I followed the path that was chosen for me: people-pleasing. Pleasing my parents ensured they were paying attention to me. Both of them were so young, but they did what they could with what they had. My mother turned 20 just a month prior to giving birth. My father, a 24-year-old man, was just beginning his journey. It's difficult to navigate parenthood when you have demons lurking inside. Memories of my biological mother are very few and far between. My parents were married and divorced in less than two years. When my father remarried I was given the opportunity for a life unlike before. However, the pain and wonderment of why my biological mom left was confusing, leaving a yearning for a mother who discarded her child. If I wasn't good enough for her then something must truly be wrong with me. Childhood trauma leaves an imprint on the brain. The scars left behind by our parents are sometimes invisible to others. I spent my childhood always looking for the acceptance of others, constantly comparing myself. Conformity over truth was my chosen path. It was far less exhausting than being authentic.

Generations before mine raised children to be obedient; to behave and do as they were told. Following these rules and guidelines set by elders simply leads to the cycle repeating. The painful cycle of pleasing those who love you leaves the soul depleted and lacking the care necessary to grow as humans. But more importantly, SELF CARE is the basis of life. If we are navigating life for the comfort of others, the soul is left quite lost. You simply cannot pour from an empty glass.

Fitting into a mold of set expectations will keep you living in a very small world. I found myself emulating others to make sure I stayed in my tiny space. From a very young age, I was intrigued by how females carried themselves. A pure essence and aura shine when a woman is in their true existence. It's uncanny. It can be spotted from afar and felt when in their presence. It's truly a beautiful thing. I found myself more interested in my best girlfriends than the boys in the *Seventeen* magazines. I became friends with all the boys because we seemed to have the most in common. But this was the early 90's and I was a church girl. Our family was very active in the local church. I sang in the choir and went to Sunday school weekly. I was baptized in the Catholic faith and then confirmed Christian in my early teens. But that was the conformity and pleasing I was trained for, not my beliefs. I would attend birthday parties and gay panic would set in playing silly games like "spin the bottle". Sometimes it would land on the most popular girl in school. Then you were required to KISS them. That was an eye-opener. Not enough to cue me of the extreme turn of events that would occur 25 years later.

Living a life designed by others never sat well with me. Severe anxiety and depression began to take control of every day. My teenage years led to rebellion and I unconsciously gave pieces of myself to undeserving people, attempting to recreate a connection I was missing. Mentally and physically, at school and work, and with family and friends - every aspect of my life was for someone else. Tearing myself down quicker than I could pick up the pieces.

Remember the three loves theory? If mapped out on the timeline of life one would expect the first of the three loves to be a young love - "puppy love". Maybe this is your first crush. The first person to hold your hand. Possibly a first kiss. The firsts are always so exciting and special. The elusive butterflies felt in those first moments are something you cannot explain, yet everyone knows the feeling. Again we are taught from a young age this feeling is good. And that this feeling is love. First encounters with love typically fade and change quickly. The second of the three loves might be construed as your teenage love. The person you get through the tough, awkward, teenage times with. A best friend really. Some find this is the person they want by their side. Some unfortunately crash and burn.

You know when you meet another person and have this insane unspoken chemistry? Instantly, like magnets, you are drawn to one another. Entire conversations through simple eye contact. Intense amounts of energy from being present in the same space. When your bodies meet, heartbeats become synced. Two souls forever tangled. I am convinced not everyone gets to experience this feeling. This is a once-in-a-lifetime connection, leaving an imprint impossible to erase. Soulmates. The thing is, a young twenty-something-year-old mind is not mature, not prepared to face deciding the path of the rest of our lives. A connection of this caliber can be unwavering in a young mind. Torn to pieces, I closed the door and left it all behind.

Life will always give you another path.

My ex-husband and I married about a year after that door closed. We went on to have two children right away. I was now a mother. I instantly realized I had no idea what I was doing. So I conformed to the housewife/mother role I had chosen. I watched other moms, and read countless materials on parenting and raising children. Usually, I found solitude with moms who were like me. Mothers who also felt lost. Without even realizing it, I was people-pleasing the world around me. This was a familiar place to be, though. I learned this tactic from childhood. Trying to be the person others wanted - or so I thought.

This included my then-husband. Living up to his standards was, quite frankly, impossible. Yet I gave it my everything. Like every marriage, there were good and bad times. That is what we signed up for after all. It takes two though. Both parties must be present emotionally, mentally, and physically. Relationships require consistency, communication, and compassion. Resentment stems from the lack of a trusting foundation and proper communication. How else are we to perceive one another? Playing guessing games about what the next tribulation holds is nonsensical. Ultimately, this festering resentment turns dark, leaving behind a jaded heart.

The spring before celebrating our 13th wedding anniversary I was faced with losing my closest friend. The details were entirely too painful to grasp. The sheer shock and disbelief were life-altering. There is no way of knowing how the brain will cope with sudden loss and grief. Providing a loved one with patience, understanding, and a safe place to land is crucial in times of crisis. I desperately needed space and time to sort flooding thoughts. To feel the anger burning inside. Everyone processes loss differently; only time can separate us from the pain.

That summer left me feeling unsure about my future, learning firsthand just how quickly everything can change. This was quite pivotal in my own personal growth. I had never felt comfortable in my own skin, struggling with disordered eating and body dysmorphia from early on. Years upon years of self-deprecation.

It was then I decided to take a look at why I was so miserable. I'd been married for 13 years, had two incredible children, and lived in a decent home. The typical suburban happily ever after. Remember? The happily ever after? I had accomplished what I was striving towards. It checked all the boxes. Except one; I was not being true to myself. The work began then. I was conditioned to compartmentalize, putting things on a shelf in the back of my mind. Safekeeping for later. Never addressing the underlying issue. Sitting with the uncomfortable feelings from my past was absolutely necessary at this juncture in life. My unhappiness was in MY hands. It didn't take but a few months to fully come out to myself. At 38 years old, I realized I am queer. Trust me, I wish I had known 20+ years prior. If you know me, maybe there were signs? All jokes aside; an entire generation of women were raised with a purpose: to make good little wives and mothers. This sounds like a generalization; however, more and more women my age are coming out later in life with the notion of compulsory heterosexuality being discussed more openly.

Accessibility of materials such as *Compulsory Heterosexuality and Lesbian Existence* written in 1980 by Adrienne Cecile or the popular 'Am I a lesbian?' masterdoc.pdf. Comphet is not new. Openly discussing it is. It's up to the LGBTQ+ community to keep speaking - LOUDLY. Doing so will allow more people to become their true selves. The LGBTQ+ community has surrounded people like me with the love needed to finally feel safe; safety and a sense of not being alone on your life journey. I am proud to break these standards whilst raising my children, teaching them to be themselves and stay true to their dreams. Leading a life they created, not a life lived for others. You only live once is so cliche, but if we don't truly know what's next, then all we have is now.

Repeat that. **All we have is now.**

Year 13 of marriage is when it all finally crumbled. No longer able to carry the immense weight of lies, deceit, and destruction.

When you feel like things are falling into place, life will give you yet another path. Then give you no choice but to walk directly into the storm.

By the fall of that year, my health had begun to decline. Others in my life thought it was stress-related. *Maybe they're right?* I thought. I had been overworking myself. At a routine check-up earlier in the year my general practitioner did a breast exam. There was a small lump. She said it was nothing to be concerned about. Women my age get lumps and bumps. Doctors continued to brush off my symptoms. In September blood labs came back abnormal. My energy level plummeted. The lump in my breast had doubled in size. It was painful but I kept going and continued to work harder than ever.

In November a CT scan revealed the mass in my right breast. It was not small anymore. I kept telling them I felt it - nobody listened. They performed a mammogram and ultrasound the week before Thanksgiving. After the test was finished I was asked to step into this small room in the back. I sat in a comfy chair against one wall with a table nearby. A box of Kleenex sat on the table. As I walked through the door alone the nurse asked me to sit down, I knew what she was about to say. This wasn't a normal appointment protocol. They call her the "nurse navigator" for a reason. She's about to schedule all of your appointments for you because you most likely have cancer.

The mammogram results were posted on the app the following day -

"IMPRESSION: SUSPICIOUS ABNORMALITY-MODERATE CONCERN BUT NOT CLASSIC FOR MALIGNANCY. The 1 cm oval mass in the right breast has a differential diagnosis of carcinoma or a fibroadenoma and is at a high suspicion for malignancy. An ultrasound-guided biopsy is recommended. BI-RADS 4c."

They tell you not to Google anything. Tell you not to worry and dwell and send you on your way with this information so nonchalantly.

The nurse navigator scheduled my biopsy for December 2nd. My family and friends did their best to keep me from unraveling. But I had already started to spiral. We were all familiar with my history of mental illness, but this episode was different. My mind had switched. I felt it happening over the course of a few weeks while I waited for that December 2nd biopsy appointment. One day I looked my ex in the eyes and begged him to call my parents; I didn't know what else to do.

My mind was slipping. I couldn't bear to let my children watch their mother lose her mind. My mom took me to the behavioral health hospital where I willingly checked myself in.

The day of my biopsy was long. There was a scheduling mistake that pushed my procedure way back. I sat in a stupid pink shirt gown for five hours that day. The procedure for guided biopsy is to watch on the ultrasound screen. The room grew very quiet. We watched the mass on the screen as they punch-biopsied my breast with a 12g needle. *These are professionals at the Women's Center,* I thought to myself, *they must know.* They have seen this so many times. It's fucking cancer.

My intuitions have never failed me. I know my body well and something was very wrong. The biopsy resulted in a diagnosis of Invasive Ductal Carcinoma. I had breast cancer at 38 years old.

The time spanning from December 2nd to my surgery on December 30th, 2021 is a blur. My family came together and created a Christmas I was unable to provide for my children. I continued to attend intensive outpatient therapy daily until the day of my first mastectomy. Yes, first.

The decision to hack off a body part is extremely difficult when you're already uncomfortable with your body. My mother and I attended an appointment with the plastic surgeon. This surgeon would install breast implants. She held this thick plastic expander while explaining it would have to be temporarily installed to stretch my skin, making room for an implant. This chunky piece of plastic looked like some kind of torture device. It all felt wrong. However, the person I had spent 13+ years with was telling me otherwise. The consensus was I would hate my body worse with no breasts. I would regret not getting implants. You see, I had small titties. What was the difference if they just weren't there? After countless mental breakdowns surrounding this decision, I decided it was best to just get the cancer out. Remove only the right side.

One of the days I was having a meltdown on my parents' kitchen floor, my mom said: "It's like when the Titanic sank. That boat had little compartments on the underside to carry water in case it sprung a leak. But once they were all full, the boat sank anyway. You are so good at keeping your compartments full. Your cancer diagnosis has filled that last compartment and your ship is sinking."

My mother's methodical, Virgo mind had nailed it. Smart lady.

I sunk my own battleship. Thanks, Mom. This is why she's the matriarch of our family. She's held it together through it all. Through my father's testicular cancer diagnosis 20 years ago, getting two daughters through college out of state, and health issues and surgeries. Everything. That woman carries it all, exhibiting a level of selflessness I admire. She takes care of my father, who took full custody of me at 18 months old when my biological mother chose addiction over her firstborn. He saved me. He is my biggest fan and supporter. My sister and I brag about how our parents are unsurpassable.

Surgery day came and went. The mass in my right breast had grown to 13mm by then but luckily did not make it to my lymph nodes. I did not require chemotherapy and have chosen to forgo the five-year hormonal treatment plan. Within a few months I "recovered" from surgery and was ready to begin life again. Whatever that meant. Now I had one breast and had to learn to view my new body. It just didn't feel "right". After a summer of having one breast in a bathing suit and tank tops, I contacted my breast surgeon. We scheduled a second mastectomy for the fall. Almost exactly a year later my left breast was removed, Aesthetic Flat Closure is the best choice I made in my cancer journey. I finally feel free. Flat and free.

Hopefully, you are wondering, what is the third love of the three loves theory? I'll leave this to your own interpretation. However, I'd like to think one of the three loves must be SELF - pure and simple self-love and care. It's basic survival. We as humans base our happiness on so many physical things. Tangible items, how we appear to others, and how we speak and interact with people in the world. Having a strong sense of self is fundamental. Without the care of our own body and soul, we are just vessels roaming this earth. Stay firmly grounded in you. But don't forget to give some wiggle room; we are all still growing.

# PART 2:
# Healing & Building Healthy Connections

Intimacy and sexuality are at the core of our human experience, woven into the fabric of our lives with sacred significance. But when these tender aspects are violated, boundaries breached, and trust shattered, the impact can be profound, leaving us feeling fractured, defeated, and adrift.

As a survivor myself and a mother to survivors, I intimately understand the damaging effects of such experiences. But instead of succumbing to victimization, we are here to offer a different path – one of acknowledgment, healing, and empowerment.

In this section, we address the journey of healing from sexual trauma, learning to embrace self-love in the aftermath of infidelity, and creating strong and healthy boundaries in the face of domestic violence. It is our sincere hope that through these candid conversations and insightful tools, you'll discover the strength to reclaim your sense of self, heal your wounds, and create a life that celebrates the beauty and sensuality that lies within you.

## Jennifer Williams

Jen's Life Coaching, LLC
Life Coach

jenslifecoaching.com
www.facebook.com/JensLifeCoaching
www.instagram.com/jens.life.coaching/

Jennifer Williams is an inspiring personal development coach helping moms all over the world reach their fullest potential. She is trauma-informed and passionate about guiding her clients through self-discovery tools, helping them learn new habits, and discovering their life purpose to create meaningful, fulfilling lives without sacrificing their children or themselves. She is on a mission to help as many women as possible feel intrinsically beautiful, independent, and confident so they aren't jealous or comparing themselves to others. As a divorced mom, Jen understands the challenges of the co-parenting territory and offers unique insight and advice to her coaching clients. Her engaging personality and compassionate approach make her a highly sought-after coach in her field. In addition to her successful private coaching practice, she is an author. Purchase Jennifer's other book, "I am Amazing, from Invisible to Invincible" on Amazon or find her growing eBooks and blog on her website today.

# EMBRACING FEMALE SEXUALITY AND EXPRESSION

By Jennifer Williams

Are you ready to explore the forbidden?

I love sex. I am an unapologetic lover of all things sexual. I crave it, I embrace it, and I can indulge in it for hours with the right person. Gender doesn't matter to me; I've had sexual encounters with both men and women.

And the adventure continues! From total strangers to dear friends, and even those late-night connections, I've fearlessly delved into the depths of my desires. No shame, just pure exploration.

But I wasn't always like this. I used to feel ashamed of my sexuality and past traumas centered around it. I felt dirty, tainted, and broken. As much as I wanted sex and physical intimacy, part of me was repulsed by it. It felt more like a chore.

Today, I celebrate my inner vixen without shame or fear of judgment. I've embraced my sexuality, and it's empowered me to express myself fully and heal past sexual trauma in ways I never thought possible. It's where I find a deep connection with my femininity, a sense of freedom to be vulnerable and explore my desires without restraint.

In a world where taboos and stigma surrounding female sexuality persist, it is crucial for women to embrace their sexual authenticity. This chapter will examine the impact of societal taboos on female sexual expression, the benefits of healing sexual trauma, the profound connection between love and sex, and the importance of fostering trust and embracing unique expressions of love. So, if you are ready to break free from the chains of society, unlock your true sexual self, and embark on a transformative journey of personal growth, read on to discover the key to embracing sexual authenticity.

Prepare yourself for an ultimate act of submission….to yourself.

## Understanding the Impact of Societal Taboos & Stigmas

Sexuality: the enigmatic force that defines who we are. It's raw, primal, and yes, even a little wild. But here's the thing - it's perfectly natural. In fact, it's one of our fundamental needs as humans, and denying that is almost like denying ourselves air.

For centuries, women who were sexually active outside the confines of marriage were shamed and ostracized, often left to wear a metaphorical "Red Letter 'A'" to denote their supposed promiscuity. It's hard to forget Nathanial Hawthorne's controversial *The Scarlet Letter*, which portrayed an unmarried woman raising a child alone as sinful and morally corrupt for her sexual choices. She and her child were punished, shamed, judged, and isolated by her community for years.

A century later, the 1960s were a revolutionary time for women's sexual expression and empowerment. From the introduction of the birth control pill to an increase in women's participation in the workforce, women were no longer confined to strict gender roles. More importantly, women were able to express themselves without judgment or societal pressure. This era paved the way for future generations of women to continue to break down barriers and embrace their sexual empowerment.

Understanding the impact of societal taboos is essential when it comes to exploring female sexual expression and embarking on a journey of personal growth. These taboos have long held women back from fully embracing their sexuality and have created a barrier to healing from past traumas. By acknowledging and challenging these societal constraints, women can begin to regain their power and find the freedom to express love through sex in their own unique ways.

These stigmas surrounding female sexuality have also had a significant impact on the healing process for survivors of sexual trauma. In a society that often blames victims or shames them into silence, it can be incredibly challenging for survivors to find the support and understanding they need to heal. By breaking down societal taboos and creating a culture of empathy and acceptance, we can create a safe space for survivors to heal their wounds, so they can explore their sexuality and reclaim their bodies.

Slowly but surely, women are reclaiming their bodies and sexual experiences, and society has evolved enough to recognize and celebrate this. It's time to end the stigma of female sexuality and acknowledge the progress we have made. We still have a long way to go, but every step counts towards a world where women can be proud of and confident in their sexuality...trauma and all. It's empowering to see how far we've come and how much we still have the potential to grow. By embracing female sexuality and ending the stigmas that come with it, we're paving the way for a brighter, sex-positive future.

## Sexual Trauma and the Effects on Intimacy

Sexual trauma is unfortunately all too common, with about 1 in 4 girls and 1 in 13 boys in the United States experiencing sexual abuse under the age of eighteen. According to Rainn.org, (Rape, Abuse & Incest National Network), America's largest anti-sexual violence organization, an American is sexually assaulted every 68 seconds.

Sexual trauma is a soul-shattering ordeal that scars us to the core. It leaves behind a deep-rooted mark on our sense of self and tampers with our ability to embrace our sexuality wholeheartedly. Tragically, countless survivors are imprisoned by shame and guilt, forced to endure their anguish in silence. The consequences? A cascade of darkness encompassing depression, anxiety, addiction, PTSD, migraines, obesity, and shattered relationships to name a few.

## My Story

When I was between nine and fourteen years old, I was sexually abused by four men. The men would touch me inappropriately, and force me to perform sexual acts on them. The first one was a neighbor and husband of my mother's friend at the time. My mother was known for being too trusting, and her ability to judge character wasn't great.

The first time it happened, when he placed his hands between my legs to "warm them up," I instinctively knew something was wrong. I was petrified. We were in the car by ourselves, and I was too terrified to tell him to stop. I moved to the passenger side and looked out the window at the sky, praying to get home quickly.

Instead, he took me to his parents' house, who were not home then. It was a few days from my ninth birthday, and he told me he needed to check my pants size to buy me some new clothes as a birthday present, and asked if he could unbutton them to look. I knew he was lying, but obliged to his request out of pure fear. I didn't want him to do this, yet I stayed silent. He pulled my pants down and quietly told me to lie on the bed. I laid down on my stomach, thinking that would protect my genitals from his advances. He didn't protest. He pinned me down, thrusting his rock-hard penis against my backside as he moaned with pleasure in my ear. I don't recall anything else after that moment, but it wasn't the last instance.

I finally found the courage to speak up and tell my mom. I vaguely remember that conversation. I don't think she believed me, because although he never touched me again, she didn't stop him from coming around me. Three other men hurt me after that. I never spoke up again, out of shame and fear, that I wouldn't be heard.

The impact of this trauma on my life has been truly overwhelming. It has left me battling anxiety, depression, weight gain, and post-traumatic stress disorder. And it has deeply affected my ability to connect intimately with others well into adulthood. It prohibited my sexual desires and created a barrier in sexual relationships.

## The Journey Towards Sexual Healing

When we experience something traumatic, it can be tempting to try and push it deep down, hoping to forget and move on. However, repressing trauma is not a viable solution and can have long-lasting consequences.

The body and our subconscious are incredible organs that are hard at work even when we're asleep. They don't forget anything, no matter how much we try. Simply because we stop consciously thinking about it does not mean our bodies have moved on too. The unhealed trauma ultimately manifests in long-term side effects like headaches, anxiety, and depression. Therefore, it's essential to address our trauma head-on, no matter how challenging or painful it may be. We must allow ourselves to feel and confront our feelings to experience true healing.

The first step in embracing my sexuality was to let go of the shame and judgment that surrounded sex and my past. Society teaches us that women who enjoy sex are "sluts" and "whores," while men who do the same thing are praised as studs by all genders. It took a lot of self-reflection and unlearning these harmful beliefs, but once I did, I found that embracing my sexuality was incredibly liberating. I could experience pleasure on my terms and without fear of being judged.

Sexual trauma creates a wound that can linger long after the event has passed. It's like an uninvited guest that refuses to leave, taking up residence in our minds and hearts. But what if we could evict this guest through forgiveness? It may seem daunting and counterintuitive at first, but forgiveness has been shown to have a powerful healing effect on trauma survivors. By releasing our anger and resentment towards our perpetrators, we create space for healing and growth.

It doesn't mean we have to excuse their behavior or forget what happened, but it does mean we can move forward with greater peace and acceptance. Forgiveness can be a difficult process, but it is worthwhile and has the potential to transform our lives.

I endured the unbearable agony of forgiving the men who caused me harm. But the most heart-wrenching journey was forgiving my own mother who failed to shield me from such individuals due to her ignorance and neglect.

I empowered myself by embracing forgiveness. It allowed me to cultivate a sense of emotional and physical security with my partner and gave me the freedom to enjoy my sexual pleasure, both giving and receiving.

Education also plays a crucial role in healing sexual trauma. By educating ourselves and others about the nature of trauma and its effects on a person's sexuality, we can promote understanding and compassion. This includes learning about the various therapies and resources available to survivors, such as trauma-informed therapy or alternative healing practices like mindfulness and meditation. We can make a difference through advocacy, awareness, and actively confronting victim-blaming attitudes. Together, we can make real change and support those who have experienced trauma.

It can be difficult to navigate feelings of shame and guilt surrounding past experiences. If you've experienced trauma, it's important to remember that healing has no timeline. Taking things slow, seeking therapy, and open communication with your partner can all help create a safe and comfortable environment where you can explore your sexuality on your own terms and at your own pace.

## Channeling Healing and Love Through Sexual Expression

Now let's talk about my favorite area of intimacy. The mind-blowing, and the most thrilling act of all. It lies in creating an electrifying, unbreakable connection with my partner. It is in this sacred realm where only we exist, a clandestine bubble where outsiders dare not enter. Our bond is forged through trust, love, patience, and the most intimate of connections. Here, we can express, explore, and indulge in pleasure. This is a place where our bodies and souls intertwine, where the healing of past and present takes place, fueled by its intoxicating power. Before healing my trauma, I could not experience this.

Sexual expression and intimacy can be powerful tools in healing past wounds and traumas when shared with a loving and understanding partner. As consenting adults, we have the right to decide what we do with our own bodies, and finding a partner who respects and supports that autonomy can be transformative. It's important to prioritize communication and understanding in any intimate relationship and to approach sexual expression as a way to connect deeply with our partners and explore our own desires and healing journeys. By embracing intimacy in this way, we can cultivate a profound sense of healing, growth, and joy.

Non-conventional sexual practices such as BDSM, KINK, and sexual role-playing can also be beneficial in fostering intimacy and trust with our partners. These practices require a lot of communication, consent, and trust, which can deepen our connection and understanding of each other's needs. It's important to remember that these practices should never feel like an obligation, and should only be explored if both partners are fully comfortable and willing.

Furthermore, trust allows for the development of a shared language of consent and mutual understanding. Each partner's boundaries and comfort levels are respected, and consent becomes an ongoing and enthusiastic conversation. This creates a dynamic where consent is not just a one-time agreement, but a continuous process of checking in and ensuring both partners are fully engaged and comfortable. By fostering trust, couples can create a space to safely explore their sexual desires.

Embracing and honoring our sexuality can also help us build trust and intimacy with our partners. When we are open and honest about our needs and desires, we create a space for vulnerability and connection. Intimacy is not just physical; it's emotional, intellectual, and spiritual. Sex can allow us to connect more deeply and foster feelings of trust and security.

When it comes down to it, the most important thing to remember on your sexual journey is that your body belongs to you. It's important to embrace your sexuality in a way that feels true to yourself and your desires. Don't let anyone else's judgment or stigma hold you back from experiencing pleasure and forming meaningful connections with others.

## In Closing

Sexual empowerment is an ongoing journey. While there is no one-size-fits-all approach to embracing womanhood and sexuality, it can be a necessary part of self-acceptance, trust, vulnerability, and connection. Sexuality is an integral part of who we are, and it's important to reclaim our story.

As women, we can counter the shame, judgment, and stigma put on female sexuality by embracing our desires and becoming agents of change in our own lives.

By learning to trust ourselves and communicate authentically and openly with others, we open up a world of possibilities for trusting relationships. It requires patience, open communication with our partners, self-reflection, and healing from past traumas. True sexual empowerment comes from within us and encourages feelings of freedom. By adopting a mindset of openness towards pleasure and exploration, plus letting go of judgment both towards ourselves and others, we can make great strides in this journey. Through self-acceptance and owning our power, we will find true sexual pleasure grounded in respect, consent, care, and love. Let's celebrate our freedom, honor each other's journeys, and create a culture of acceptance within ourselves and among others. Together, we can create a society where sexual liberation is the norm.

## Anonymous

Hello and Welcome! Such a great opportunity has been presented through co-authoring for *Womanhood: Identity to Intimacy and Everything In Between!* To be able to connect and empower other women's journeys as we share our stories is priceless. It is my hope that my story reaches those who think they have been destroyed by abuse. You are not alone! There is hope and love waiting for you. Because you deserve better! Your journey to happiness begins within you!

# INNOCENCE LOST

By Anonymous

*Everyone has a story, and my intention in sharing mine is to offer hope, healing, and strength to those who have endured deeply disturbing experiences. While the content of my story may be uncomfortable, I hope you can find a path to clarity, forgiveness, and resilience.*

*To those who have survived sexual abuse, I admire your courage in reading this chapter. I hope it can serve as a source of guidance and reassurance, reminding you that you are not alone.*

## Facing the Reality: Childhood Sexual Abuse Statistics

According to the National Sexual Violence Resource Center, approximately 1 in 9 girls under the age of 18 experience sexual abuse or assault at the hands of an adult. These numbers are not just statistics; they represent countless lives forever altered by the trauma of abuse.

Often abusers are individuals known to the victim. In fact, studies have shown that in about 90% of reported cases, the abuser is someone within the victim's circle of trust, such as a family member, family friend, or caregiver.

Abusers are skilled manipulators, experts at hiding their actions behind a facade of normalcy and trustworthiness. Add to this the heart-wrenching reality that victim-blaming and shaming causes many victims to stay silent. And it's a grim paradox that, too often, when children *do* muster the courage to speak up, they are brushed off, or worse - accused of lying. They then have to bear the agony of listening to their abuser being unfairly defended, perpetuating the cycle of silence and suffering.

But the cycle stops here.

It's time to open up those conversations, reclaim our voices, and shine light into the darkness. The story we're about to share is, regrettably, the living nightmare of far too many girls. We share it here to break the silence.

## The Seeds of Resilience

As I embarked on planting seeds in my garden this past Spring, I had a realization about the resilience of the human mind. Just as seeds thrive under the right conditions, our mental well-being can flourish with proper care. When we nurture, tend to, and nourish the seeds, we reap a bountiful harvest. So, too, do we grow when we are nurtured, tended to and nourished.

However, when subjected to neglect or overwhelming stress, our emotional growth can suffer. Abuse, in particular, can have a detrimental impact on our psychological development. I strongly encourage seeking professional therapy if you are struggling with the aftermath of abuse. It's common to bury the pain, only to have it resurface in unexpected ways.

## A Summer of Deception

In the summer of '69, I became a part of my family, which included two older brothers, my mother, and my father. The neighborhood welcomed me with a celebration, and everyone was genuinely excited to have me join this upper-middle-class, church-oriented, and community-minded family. Interestingly, our Sheltie, Prince, who typically didn't like children, made an exception for me. It's a reminder that animals have an intuitive sense of whether someone is friendly. I wish humans had this trait.

As my family embraced me, my father took on the role of nighttime caregiver while my mother tended to my older brothers' needs. On the surface, it seemed like a loving and innocent bonding time, with baths, lullabies, and bedtime stories. However, beneath the façade, he was grooming me for what he called "special massages," a dark secret we shared. I believed that no one else would understand our connection, and he convinced me that revealing this secret would mean the end of our special time together.

Our favorite nursery game, "Where is Thumbkin?" had a disturbing twist, as one of my father's "thumbs" was bigger and always remained visible. Diaper changing became a traumatic event where he threatened me with a safety pin if I cried or squirmed, ultimately subjecting me to inappropriate touching. I quietly submitted though I couldn't comprehend why my father, who claimed to love me, would cause me such pain.

My mother occasionally inquired about the commotion, but my father deftly dismissed any concerns. Dad was sneaky and said I was just squirming and was accidentally pricked by the pin. Mom suggested I was old enough to put myself to sleep, yet the routine continued. I did not know why I had been punished. I blamed myself for not pleasing him enough. I felt abandoned, shunned, and disconnected since this was the only attention he gave me most days.

## The Shadows of Coping

As the abuse continued, I developed a coping mechanism of dissociation, mentally distancing myself from the torment. I sought refuge in my imagination, where I created safe havens to escape the horrors of reality. Personality disorders emerged, and I began acting out.

Emotionally, I shut down and withdrew, resisting attempts by my brothers to control me, fearing they might hurt me too. This internal turmoil persisted into my adolescence.

My mother was a nurturing and loving source of comfort. I became deeply reliant on her approval, constantly seeking ways to earn her favor. Disappointment was not just disheartening but rather devastating, leading me to steer clear of trying new things out of the fear of failing – a trait that persisted throughout my entire life.

I dreaded the idea of having my opinions brushed off with a mere, "Well, I don't know about that," or even worse, met with no response at all, just a blank, blinking stare as if my words were swiftly assessed and then summarily dismissed. The absence of validation left me feeling helpless, and I eventually gave up attempting to articulate how I felt and what I thought. I began to lock away my emotions and thoughts, keeping them hidden deep within.

When I started experiencing puberty, my mother gave me a health book, instructing me to read it and ask questions if needed. Despite my awareness of the biology of reproduction, I was emotionally unprepared for what I was experiencing. I despised my changing body, and taunts from my family about being "chubby" worsened my self-image. I felt ugly and undesirable. Sexuality was scary and I avoided any potential boyfriends. I kept my attire boyish and loose so as not to draw attention to my changing body. Yet, my dad was increasingly trying to catch a glimpse of me naked and making inappropriate comments like, "Hey, why don't you put your bikini on?" His suggestions made me uncomfortable and nauseous, but my mom shrugged it off and told me I didn't have to wear it if I didn't want to, but that I looked cute in it so why not?

One day my mom told me she had a dream about me and a man having sex behind the couch. I was 12. I swore to her that was never going to happen. She said, "All I know is that your birth mother was young when she had you. I do not want you to end up like her."

And there it was. I was adopted.

Different, not "special," and destined to become a teenage mother. My mom was placing her paranoia on me to protect my virtue. It made me feel dirty and unworthy of a valid, healthy adulthood.

While she was obsessed with my virginity, I was searching for acceptance. Alcohol became a refuge from the pain, leading to a pattern of self-destructive behavior. I engaged in risky behavior and used intoxication as an excuse for actions I later regretted. Alcohol-induced unconsciousness became a familiar state, often triggering memories of the abuse.

I maintained a childlike demeanor, seeking validation from others and avoiding failure at all costs. My fear of having my opinions dismissed or ignored led me to continue to suppress my thoughts and emotions, contributing to emotional confusion throughout my life.

In 2002, my then-husband and I sought help through Alcoholics Anonymous, which marked the beginning of my journey to sobriety. As my body healed, suppressed memories of abuse resurfaced, blurring the lines between reality and false memory. I began taking antidepressants and experienced some relief from the night terrors, but my emotional and cognitive growth lagged behind.

## Shattered Dreams and Broken Relationships

Despite nearly two decades of marriage, three children, and sobriety, my marriage eventually dissolved in 2012. This triggered a series of failed relationships and one more attempt at marriage, driven by a desperate search for external validation, ignoring warning signs and red flags, and holding onto the fantasy of love prevailing.

I gave everyone else what I was so desperately craving - unconditional love. I gave so much to others that I neglected my own needs. This pattern left me emotionally depleted, eventually leading to a mental breakdown that resulted in my hospitalization.

While seeking treatment I experienced an unwanted sexual advance that unlocked a floodgate. In that vulnerable moment, my repressed memories returned vividly, confirming the abuse I had endured.

In isolation, I shared my truth with the staff at the mental institution and began to process the trauma, but my primary concern was how my family would react - especially my mother.

My mom came to visit me and I shared my experience with her. She accepted my version of my truth, but couldn't understand how the abuse could happen without her knowledge. I said, "Because you did not want to know. Who would? You did as you were taught just as I did. To respect, accept, and love unconditionally."

She asked me why I had never told her. I explained, as a coping mechanism I had suppressed the memories of the abuse. I hid those emotions from everyone including myself. She hugged me and told me she believed me. That she would have done something if she knew. That she had a suspicion but nothing solid, so she let it go.

Today, I choose to let it go.

## A Healing Farewell

Currently, with the support of therapy, appropriate medication, and a strong support system, I work as a health advisor, helping others achieve their wellness goals through natural products. Helping people awaken to become who they are meant to be: their best!

This was one of my dad's sayings:, "It's the best." It makes me laugh now when I think of all the energy and mind games he had to play to maintain his delusional image.

My dad recently passed. I had visited him once in the assisted living center. I told him I forgave him but would not forget the abuse. He continued to deny all accounts, saying, "I cannot have this said about me. What will others think?" Perception was always his strong point. Or so, he thought. But reality and truth prevail as healers.

Before his cremation I said a release-of-negativity ritual, wrote him a poem and said my peace. It was one of forgiveness which released me from the bondage of victimization. I sent him off with a song and prayer, hoping that he finds peace.

## The Blooming Garden of Resilience

As I stand in my garden, tending to the vibrant flowers that now surround me, I am reminded of the seeds of resilience that were planted. They may take my body, but my mind is my own. There is no room for hate or acts of revenge. This blocks love for others and me. Today that comes first.

In sharing my story, I hope to inspire women and all survivors to find their inner strength, seek healing, and embrace the power of forgiveness. Our past may shape us, but it does not define us. We can bloom beyond the shadows, just like the resilient seeds in a garden, thriving under the right conditions.

Together, we can cultivate a future filled with love, support, and empowerment for all.

Recognizing the signs of abuse and being there for someone who discloses such trauma is crucial. Understand that abusers are often very skilled at manipulating and hiding their actions. They may groom their victims, using tactics to gain trust and silence their victims' voices. As a society, we must prioritize the safety and well-being of our children. If you suspect abuse, trust your instincts, and report your concerns to the appropriate authorities. If someone you know discloses abuse, listen without judgment, offer support, and believe their story. Your role can be instrumental in helping them heal and seek justice.

One of the most critical aspects of addressing childhood sexual abuse is taking the victim's disclosure seriously. Mothers, in particular, play a vital role in ensuring their children's safety. If your child comes to you with an allegation of abuse, it is paramount that you **listen, believe**

**them, and take immediate action to protect them.** This includes reporting the abuse to the authorities and seeking professional help for your child.

Remember that your reaction can shape their healing journey. Take their words seriously, seek professional help, and support them unconditionally. By doing so, you can be the anchor that helps them navigate the turbulent waters of recovery.

## Brandi Liberty

CEO of The Luak Group

www.luakgroup.com
brandiliberty.wixsite.com/soulfulechoes
www.linkedin.com/in/brandiliberty
www.facebook.com/profile.php?id=100076986827441&mibextid=L
QQJ4d
www.instagram.com/nola_ioway_girl/?

Brandi Liberty, enrolled member of the Iowa Tribe of Kansas and Nebraska and descendent of the United Houma Nation, has a profound dedication to tribal communities and a diverse professional background encompassing tribal development, strategic planning, and domestic violence advocacy. As the CEO of The Luak Group, she's championed grant writing, tribal community planning, tribal housing, and safeguarding tribal sovereignty while securing over $78 million in grant awards for tribal communities. Brandi's journey as a survivor of domestic violence through narcissistic abuse propelled her into advocacy, where she presented as a keynote presenter on personality disorders and abuse. She holds an MA from the Center of Indigenous Nations Studies at the University of Kansas and an Executive Leadership Certificate from Harvard Business School's Leading People and Investing to Build Sustainable Communities Program through NAFOA. Brandi is an empowered single mom to two amazing children.

# LOVE, LOSS, AND RESILIENCE: RELATIONSHIPS AFTER HEARTBREAK

By Brandi Liberty

My perception of love has evolved many times over the course of my life. Initially, I mistook a narcissistic partner's deceptive performance for genuine love, leading me to lose my identity and my self-worth. Over the past decade, every relationship I have had has reshaped my understanding of love, from the friendship kind of love to intimate partner love. We all have distinct tales of love and heartbreak, yet they resonate in a collective human experience. Our heartbreaks, embedded with emotions known only to ourselves experiencing them shape our past, present, and future selves. While love, loss, and resilience remain personal in their notion to the individual, nothing quite parallels the profound pain of the universal experience of heartbreak.

Raised by parents with a resilient 45-year marriage, my theory of love was shaped by both their enduring bond and the heartbreaks of their closest friends losing the loves of their lives. Although their marriage had its challenges, their unwavering love served as a beacon for many, including my own friends. My parents and some of their friends were my early role models in love. As I matured, I experienced my own tales of love, loss, and profound resilience—whether from losing a dear friend to cancer or supporting others through their heartaches. Despite facing personal heartbreaks, betrayals, and challenges, I continually rise with courage, not just surviving but thriving and always extending support to those who need it.

I am a 45-year-old "Warrior Mom" and a devoted mother of two. An entrepreneur engaged in servant leadership with tribal nations, I've always been driven, striving to honor the legacy of my parents, grandparents, and ancestors. Despite my determination, I once believed "It will never happen to me".

I fell deeply for my ex, thinking it was love. Early red flags were dismissed. Our relationship sped up, and within months, we shared a home. He soon controlled my finances and social interactions. Reckless spending and theft became routine, forcing me to seek help from my parents. Six months in, I tried addressing his abusive behavior, but it worsened my emotional state. His unpredictable outbursts made me withdraw socially and live in perpetual fear, leading me further into emotional distress, and turning me into a mere shadow of my former self, filled with fear and trauma.

On one trip, he locked me in a hotel room and later returned, harming himself. Another time, he concocted a mugging story after a drunken night, which I doubted. My career ignited his jealousy, leading to relentless calls and false accusations. Ultimately, I lost my job.

During our wedding week, I juggled academics with preparations while he indulged in partying. One night, he returned inebriated, demanding intimacy. I refused, and he raged, seeking to destroy our marriage certificate which I had hidden. He also made advances on one of my closest friends, which I later found out had happened to numerous female friends, co-workers, and acquaintances. Despite the chaos, we married. After the divorce, I discarded our wedding pictures - reminders of anguish.

Our honeymoon abroad mirrored past traumas already part of the pattern: heated arguments, verbal abuse, and another episode where he locked me out of our hotel room to sleep outside on the patio. The stark realization of my plight hit me. The following year saw our relationship crumble. After the birth of our first child, he blindsided me with a notice of divorce, evicting us, seizing assets, and spreading falsehoods about me. I filed, ready to leave everything but my child behind. My lawyer identified his narcissistic tendencies, a concept foreign to me then.

To my shock, I learned I was pregnant again amidst all this. He pledged reform, and for our children, I gave him another chance. Yet, I found evidence of his online affairs through dating apps and Craigslist. Deciding my next move required careful thought; I couldn't easily leave again. Late into my second pregnancy, he again wanted a divorce, emptying our savings and demanding my earnings. No one ever filed for divorce at that time, however, a couple of weeks later, our second child was born, and we separated again, spending weeks with family in another state. We went back to him, a pattern at this point that had happened all too frequently. We faced eviction (for a second time), and together we moved to another state, but I knew it was only a matter of time before I had to release the warrior within and escape.

A year later, during what I now refer to as my own D-Day, I initiated the final divorce, and I firmly believed I was well-prepared. My therapy sessions had been extensive, and I had a basic understanding of narcissistic abuse. However, the following 14 months and the year after completely transformed my perspective on abuse, revealing aspects of my relationship I never imagined existed. My attorney highlighted the sexual abuse I had endured as I explained the previous five years. I hadn't recognized his constant demeaning, coercion, and inappropriate actions as abuse. He acted inappropriately with many women, including making unsettling remarks about children. As I went through the next year, others shared with me their harrowing experiences with him, confirming my conviction of his predatory nature.

## Personal Reflections on Infidelity

Multiple discrepancies in evidence led to a revelation that broke my silence about infidelity in my marriage. While the concept of infidelity varies across relationships, its core is deception and breaches of trust. Uncovering it feels like a profound loss, bringing a whirlwind of emotions. For me, it validated my need to exit the relationship. However, my situation wasn't just about infidelity but also narcissistic abuse. Such relationships often involve years of psychological distress before realization. The lines between reality and illusion blur, making one susceptible to further traumas. Physical abuse was absent, but discovering infidelity shattered my long-held belief against cheating, and finding the proof of infidelity broke that theory of love I had that I had told myself my entire adult life: "If infidelity happened to me, I would leave," and it prompted my departure.

## Reclaiming Self: Rising from the Ashes

In the raw tapestry of love, few threads pull as painfully as those woven by narcissistic partners. They leave behind not just heartbreak, but a profound distortion of self, a clouded perception marred by manipulation. The loss you feel as a survivor is one of relief, yet tearfully painful. To reclaim yourself, you have to find yourself...something that can take years. Yet, even from such depths of your internal hell, the human spirit can rise, resilient and empowered.

The end of a relationship, no matter how it ends, is always painful; heartbreak is inevitable for one or both individuals. But when that relationship has been with a narcissist, the wounds run deeper and are more mentally deceptive. Emotional scars, psychological trauma, and sometimes even physical marks are left behind. Remnants of a word called "love" that was more about control than care. Although I had been in therapy for the majority of my marriage, I wasn't prepared for the depths of the wounds that had clawed into every inch of my body. Even 15 years later, I still find myself healing under certain dynamics and triggers.

Gaslighting, a commonly employed tactic by narcissists, compounds the pain. This sinister strategy involves manipulating someone into doubting their reality. Over time, the victim starts questioning their sanity, memory, and their sense of self. Many people have this idea in their mind of what an abused woman looks like. They don't believe that it's someone smart and educated, someone who should know better. The woman is often victim-blamed...I found out quickly that even the most caring and understanding people have this impression. I had educated myself on narcissistic abuse over those last two years and I was able to articulate my abuse to those who asked. I could lay out the patterns of post-divorce abuse, I could outline the steps of the stalking, down to the detailed, repressed memories as they surfaced, and to this day, there are many people who don't understand the impact of what I went through. That lack of understanding only gaslights me further; having to explain the reality of it over and over leaves me questioning my insecurities and sanity at times.

## Beginning the Healing Process

Healing from such profound hurt requires acknowledgment without self-blame. It took me many years to learn this. Accepting that I was in a toxic relationship without berating myself for "not seeing the signs" or "not leaving sooner" was crucial. I blamed myself, especially where my children were concerned - a residue of the narcissist's manipulation. Recognizing this misplaced guilt for what it is becomes the first step towards healing. I've spent hours in therapy, speaking to that girl I once was, letting her know she was the strongest person I had ever met and to look how far she'd come.

Long-term therapy, especially from those knowledgeable about narcissistic abuse, played a pivotal role in my healing journey post-divorce. In the initial years, therapy was largely centered around discussing divorce-related issues since I felt I was overburdening my loved ones with my concerns. However, three years post-divorce, and after a year of no contact with the narcissist and another subsequent relationship, one therapist posed a significant question: she asked me to outline three essentials I sought from future relationships.

The first boundary was "No lying." Deception deeply unsettles me, and my intolerance for it solidified after enduring a relationship and a marriage that was riddled with deceit. In the aftermath, discerning truth from falsehood became challenging. While vestiges of my past insecurities occasionally make me doubt, I staunchly believe that openness and truthfulness form the bedrock of any relationship. A single lie can erode my trust, making me perpetually skeptical of one's authenticity.

Secondly, I had a strict "No cheating" rule. I've always believed in exclusive relationships. When I'm romantically or intimately involved with someone, my attention remains undivided, and I anticipate a similar commitment in return. If a partner wishes to pursue someone else, I'd rather they be forthright about it. While physical intimacy might cease, a friendship could persist based on mutual respect.

The last boundary was "No baby-momma-drama." My maiden relationship post-marriage involved a pre-existing child. My upbringing in a blended family provided a frame of reference for such dynamics. Despite the challenges, I was committed to emulating the love and support I had experienced. However, discord between the child's biological parents jeopardized this relationship. At that juncture, my lingering trauma from marital experiences made me reconsider. I hypothesized that perhaps dating someone childless or a widower might alleviate such issues, although both scenarios would undoubtedly come with their unique intricacies.

I later recounted these boundaries to my therapist, highlighting my apprehensions concerning relationships with individuals who had children from previous marriages. However, the universe had other plans. A year after this revelation, I entered a committed relationship with a man who had children. This relationship disproved my earlier reservations, showing me that a harmonious, blended family was attainable without the trauma I had previously associated with it. It reframed my perspective, teaching me that certain boundaries, while significant, could be approached with flexibility and discernment in varied relationship contexts.

## Rebuilding My Self-Worth

The journey to recovery began with reconstructing my damaged self-esteem. My current therapist equipped me with tools and insights, fostering a profound self-awareness of who I was and who I wanted to be. She trained me to counter the detrimental internal dialogues and the self-blame sown by the narcissistic partner. She reinforced the boundaries I'd set earlier, especially the top two, which sometimes became hazy due to past insecurities. It was essential for me to recognize even subtle boundary breaches to establish, communicate, and implement these boundaries effectively. With newfound clarity, I found it easier to assert these boundaries first in long-standing friendships. Setting boundaries is an art, tailored to individuals and circumstances. Unfortunately, some couldn't respect my boundaries, even after pointing them out to them directly, leading to their exit from my life.

Establishing boundaries and being vulnerable with intimate partners has proved more challenging. Over the past decade, I've been in two significant relationships, each nearly three years long, presenting their own sets of challenges. Interspersed between these relationships were shorter connections with intimate partners and periods of finding myself and reflection. Being an inherent extrovert, solitude often magnifies my trauma-induced anxieties. However, the company of friends and family, serving as nurturing support systems, bolstered my resilience.

I've grown weary of societal labels. Terms like "dating" and "boyfriend" seem incongruous at my age and given my experiences. For me, it's actions over titles that truly depict a relationship's nature. However, a juncture does arrive when discussing the relationship's future. Such moments demand communication, boundary definition, and vulnerability. This process isn't about rigidity; it's centered on self-respect and knowing what you want.

Admittedly, my insecurities often overshadow my decisions. The thought of dating evokes a spectrum of emotions from hope, fear, excitement, to anxiety. Acknowledging these feelings without haste has been pivotal to defining my self-worth. I constantly remind myself that while I'm a "work in progress", not everyone comprehends the reasons behind my boundaries. Nevertheless, I believe that every small triumph, like setting a boundary, deserves celebration. Although triggers persist, they no longer plunge me into a rabbit hole of despair. Prioritizing self-care, I indulge in activities that fortify my self-worth. While I relish my independence, I'm cognizant of the fact that I've weathered storms many cannot fathom. The transition from the naive girl of yesteryears to today's resilient woman and mother has been transformative. Even as the prospect of new relationships seems overwhelming, past experiences illuminate my path. Rather than approaching relationships with skepticism, I embrace them with guarded hope fortified by past lessons.

I don't know if I'll ever get to experience the same true love and resilience that I grew up with while watching my parents, and I'm okay with that. I'm not jealous of those who have had that opportunity, rather I have a profound sense of respect for them being able to take their relationships to those levels. I'm okay with not marrying again; I'm okay with finding companionship and my meaning of love. I know I'm far from never having to experience heartbreak again, but my experiences have given me the resilience to move forward no matter the situation. The wisdom I've gained from hindsight, and the empathy I've developed from personal pain, continue to guide me. I believe that the human spirit is capable of healing, growth, and finding love in whatever form they want for themselves once again.

## Kyla Biedermann

Legacy Women Affiliates LLC

legacywomenaffiliates.com/
www.facebook.com/LegacyWomenAff/
www.instagram.com/legacywomenaffiliates/

Kyla is an internationally acclaimed bestselling author, celebrated for her contributions to the renowned anthology, "Shattering the Stigma of Single Motherhood." Her illustrious career encompasses an impressive 8-year tenure in the Navy, where she served as a highly skilled Cryptologic Technician.

Through her Business, Legacy Women Affiliates, and as a member of the esteemed leadership team at She Rises Studios, Kyla uses her platform to build and support Legacy Women and her voice as a powerful tool in the ongoing fight against domestic violence.

In 2020, Kyla's life took a transformative turn when she embraced single motherhood. This experience ignited her recognition of the pressing need for a cultural shift and an alteration in attitudes towards single mothers. Driven by her determination to be the change she wished to see, Kyla embarked on a journey of healing and transformation. Her life motto is "Always Learning, Always Growing, Always Changing."

# INTIMATE INSIGHTS INTO DOMESTIC ABUSE

By Kyla Biedermann

## The Wrong Side of the Tracks

Recently I was a part of a round table discussion with a group of women discussing how we rose from the ashes of destruction in our lives. During the discussion, one of the women described being from the "wrong side of the tracks" prior to her healing journey, and a lot of us seemed to resonate with that. It immediately brought me back to my childhood, and I had a lightbulb moment. I remembered hanging out with other kids from the "wrong side of the tracks" because they had always accepted me for who I was. I remember having hatred towards the kids who did not want to be my friends and feeling resentment towards everything that defined those children and their families. They never accepted me, and I remember feeling like I was just from the wrong side of the track and that's why. My parents divorced when I was 10 and I was not brought up in the most normal household, and because of this, the observations, experiences, and attitudes that I had been exposed to were not normal and did not teach me how to form healthy relationships with other people. So it got me thinking, while I believed those kids were just mean and from the "right side of the tracks", the reality was that they had learned different behavioral traits, boundaries, attitudes, and beliefs from their families, which restricted them from acting and thinking in certain ways. This resulted in them being turned off by derelict behavior. In contrast, the kids who were fellow derelicts grew up more like me without the boundaries and restraints of acting in certain ways, and together we cultivated an environment that accepted and encouraged unhealthy beliefs and behaviors.

Many believe that you can't change who you are if you come from the "wrong side of the tracks". It's a rough environment, filled with unimaginable amounts of pain, whether it is broken relationships, job losses, addiction, trouble with the law, money problems, violence, etc., and for those who decide they deserve better and that there can be happiness, love, acceptance, and pure intimacy in life, they have to fight long and hard to take back control of their lives. They have to learn to set healthy boundaries and begin to heal from the hurt; *they have to get themselves on the right side of the tracks.* This is why eventually, those who are healing and growing begin to drift apart from their old friends, the ones who keep themselves on the "wrong side of the tracks". In order to become the person you want to be, you must surround yourself with the kind of people you want to become. Successful, thriving, women who set boundaries, have standards, hold themselves accountable, are reliable, respect others and themselves, make good choices, take responsibility for the good and the bad, constantly learn and grow into wiser more mature versions of themselves, have values, understand the consequences of their actions, and say no to things that will jeopardize success, including anything that does not cultivate a loving, caring, supportive, thriving environment.

As I write this I am a divorced, single mother who has been in a handful of abusive relationships. After each one I swore it would never happen again. I believed that no matter how I acted or what my behaviors and beliefs were, I could find love and acceptance and have a happy family life in a safe, intimate relationship. There came a point in my life where I had to accept that just saying things like, "I will never get divorced" or "I will never be in another abusive relationship" wasn't working. Blaming the individuals that had caused me pain wasn't working either. And if these situations were a coincidence and it was everyone else's fault I was in a cycle of broken relationships, how was it happening over and over again? The only logical conclusion was that these instances were a direct reflection of something I was allowing to happen in my life over and over again. Which was a hard pill to swallow. I believed I was nice and caring, and regardless of my beliefs and behaviors, I could have healthy relationships, but the relationships I was choosing and thinking were healthy were always the exact opposite of what I was looking for.

I would later come to learn all about the beliefs and behaviors I had that were making me vulnerable, but also just not making the best decisions about where I was looking and the kind of man I was looking for. So when I talk about making better decisions and taking accountability for where we are in life, I am specifically referring to making better decisions about the men we allow in our lives and the empowerment we have when we are in control of our lives and in a safe, positive environment that we are able to create for ourselves. This is really hard to do if you are self-sabotaging and have no idea where you are going wrong. We will never enjoy safe intimacy if we stay in the cycle of broken relationships. So, we are in control of ourselves, the decisions we make, and who we allow in our lives; if that relationship then becomes abusive, we no longer have control over that. It is not our fault or what we deserve at all. We have a much better chance of avoiding that happening when we decide to stop hanging around individuals who choose to stay on the "wrong side of the tracks", taking time to know ourselves and learn our vulnerabilities. Learning abuser tactics to look out for, (I only describe one in this chapter) and never stop learning and evolving into better versions of yourself. I am often reminded of Newton's third law of motion which states: "For every action, there is an equal and opposite reaction." This not only applies to motion physics, though; every choice we make will have an effect, and we have to make sure we make good decisions to get the best possible outcomes. We are always one choice away from success or failure. The only way we get better things in life is to make better decisions.

## Defining Domestic Abuse

When it comes to domestic abuse, many only think of physical abuse and oftentimes, if there is not a physical aspect to the abuse, many might believe there is no abuse happening at all. But the physical is only one aspect of it. Abuse can be physical, emotional, psychological, spiritual, financial, or sexual, and experiencing any of these ultimately abuses your time. If you think about it, these are the seven ways in which we exist as human beings. We have a physical form, each of us has our own emotions and psychological thoughts, and we have a spiritual aspect to us also. How we spend our time says a lot about who we are and what we like. We all have sexuality, and how we spend our money/resources defines our environment. Most abuse is a combination of some or all aspects of our lives and is a full-on attack on everything that makes us who we are. In fact, 95% of cases that involve physical abuse also involve emotional and psychological abuse. Even worse, these types of abuse can be done in very subtle ways which make it seem like we are overreacting or we may not even notice. This subtle abuse does not exactly send off alarm bells until it is too late and the victim is caught too deep into it. On top of that, abusers are slowly isolating you from all forms of support such as self-belief, financial security, family, friends, and anything else that gives women independence. This is why it may be hard for many to understand how women stayed or why they may not believe women when they reach out for help. Between 21-60% of abused women end up losing their jobs, which accounts for around 80 million days of work being missed yearly. Women who experience abuse not only suffer physical and mental health challenges, but they are also more likely to have sexual and reproductive health issues including being more vulnerable to developing HIV and STIs. Those who have a firearm in the household, regardless of who it belongs to, have a 500% increased risk of homicide. Currently, 1 out of 3 women have been in an abusive relationship, which is the same as it was in the 80s.

## Beliefs and Behaviors that Make Women Vulnerable and Susceptible to Abuse

How do we make ourselves attractive and susceptible to abusers? I want you to understand something very crucial. If you have been in one abusive relationship, the likelihood of you being in another one is HIGH! You may avoid them for the most part but in most cases, the reason you got into it in the first place is because of personal beliefs and behaviors you have that make you vulnerable and susceptible to abusers, and you probably don't even know it! Abusers are looking for certain kinds of women. Almost everything abusers do is testing and training to see if you would give in and fall for the façade. This is how I found myself in abusive relationships over and over again. Each time, I thought I had figured out how to avoid them, but I was actually attracting them and allowing them to be a part of my life due to my vulnerable beliefs and behaviors, coupled with my refusing to get away from the wrong crowds and making bad choices about who I was letting into my life.

The beliefs and behaviors listed in this section and the next must be credited to Dr. Dina McMillan. Her groundbreaking research on domestic abuse associates social psychology with thousands of interviews with abusers, survivors, and victims of abuse, which is why her insights and teachings are so valuable.

## Vulnerable beliefs about men:

- Masculine men are controlling
- Men are naturally more jealous than women
- Men can't be expected to understand women
- Men need sex, women don't
- All men cheat
- It's ok to date a man without a job or place to stay
- Jealous men are just being caring

- Nice guys are bland and sexually inadequate
- I'm more interested in bad guys because they are more fun
- What I really want is to be swept away by a romantic man
- I want a passionate and exciting guy
- I am looking for my happily ever after fairytale

## General vulnerable beliefs:

- I trust people until they prove they cannot be trusted
- I would rather be seen as nice instead of being too demanding and seen as angry, harsh, or mean
- Everyone deserves a second or even third chance
- Things always work out for the best
- I always see the best in people
- If someone is very insistent on something I usually give in
- It takes courage to be with someone who has a bad past
- No pain, no gain
- Suffering is part of a meaningful relationship
- You have to kiss a lot of frogs before you find a prince

## Vulnerable beliefs about self:

- I can't change my taste in men
- I have to experience things for myself to learn a lesson
- I view myself as easygoing and I really dislike being single

## Vulnerable behaviors:

- I plunge right in with someone if I feel the attraction
- Been involved with men I didn't really like because I was lonely
- Been with men I felt sorry for but did not want because of the effort they put into pursuing me
- Stayed in relationships because I had invested too much

- Returned to or stayed in a relationship because my partner threatened to hurt themselves if we broke up

## Sexual Deviancy

Intimacy is such a special thing that so many women long for. In an intimate relationship, individuals share their thoughts, feelings, fears, dreams, and desires with one another, fostering a sense of closeness and bonding which involves trust, vulnerability, mutual understanding, and a deep sense of being known and accepted by another person. However, in a relationship with an abusive partner, the concept of intimacy becomes distorted and perverted and can severely impact the ability to experience healthy intimacy, hindering the potential for a fulfilling and respectful connection. Abuse in one relationship affects how individuals will think, feel, and act in future relationships. Intimacy is the quickest way for an abuser to infiltrate and create false feelings of trust, acceptance, and vulnerability. Dr. Dina McMillan knows all too well: "The signs of an abuser will show up in the bedroom," and due to intimacy happening in such private and personal settings, it is usually "seen first in the bedroom." The other reason for this is that abusers know that the more perverse they are with women, the less likely the women are to report them due to the shame of the acts committed.

### Signs of an abuser in the bedroom include:

- Rushing to get you into bed
- Using sex as a reward or punishment
- Pushing sexual acts that make you uncomfortable
- Pushing to have sex in inappropriate places or settings
- Speaking very highly of how they "perform"
- Watching pornography
- Prodding for indecent pictures and videos

*"Sex that does not involve your wants and needs, is using you."*
—Dr. Dina McMillan

## Closing Remarks

In order to experience all that intimacy is and should be, we must treat it like the sacred experience that it is. We must see ourselves as valuable and worthy of experiencing the deepest, safest intimate connections, ones that lead to a real happy ending, a real prince, and a real fairytale. Fairytales don't happen with those whose mind is clouded by constant perverse and deviant sexual thoughts. There is a time and place for that, and a man who can't control his thoughts and lust is not someone capable of being a prince. So in the future, instead of looking for a fairytale, look for a man who makes you more holy, a man who lives in truth and wants truth for you. Look for a man who only puts you in situations that uplift you, a man who protects your reputation and innocence, a man who is genuinely focused on your growth and comfort, and a man who is slow to the bedroom and steadfastly loyal to you.

*"Love is patient and kind; love does not envy or boast; it is not arrogant or rude. It does not insist on its own way; it is not irritable or resentful; it does not rejoice at wrongdoing, but rejoices with the truth. Love bears all things, believes all things, hopes all things, endures all things."* —1 Corinthians 13:4-7

To learn more about me, and follow all my socials, check out my link tree: linktr.ee/Legacywomenaf

# PART 3:
# Motherhood Unveiled

Motherhood is an integral part of womanhood, but it's a journey that unfolds differently for each of us. Some of us choose to embrace it, while others may choose a different path. And you know what? That's absolutely okay.

Here, we have a few candid conversations about the complexities of maternal identity. We'll explore the choice of not having children, postpartum mental health and intimacy, and thriving in the dating world as a single mother.

Together, we'll begin to unveil the beauty and strength in every motherhood journey, regardless of the chosen path.

**Katie Sauer**

katiesauer1.wixsite.com/website
www.linkedin.com/in/katie-sauer-97176112b/

Katie is an aspiring author who works remotely as a Web Content Specialist. She was born and raised in Illinois but has since moved to East Tennessee with her partner (Justin) and their three cats (King, Caterpie, and Bandit).

Katie is a college graduate who obtained her Bachelor of Arts in Creative Writing and English from Southern New Hampshire University in 2020. When she is not working, she can be found with her nose in a book, volunteering at the local library, hanging out with friends, or just relaxing at home.

This is Katie's first co-author experience and she couldn't be more excited to be part of the journey! To learn more about Katie and see some of her other work visit: katiesauer1.wixsite.com/website or send her an email at 865writes@gmail.com.

# KIDS? NO THANKS.

By Katie Sauer

If you had asked me when I was in eighth grade where I saw myself in 10 years, I would have told you planning a wedding and/or planning to have children. If you were to ask me that same question at twenty-one, I would have laughed and told you, "In ten years I hope to be at peace with myself." If you asked me in eighth grade how many kids I wanted when I was older, I would have answered, "Eight." If you ask me that same question now my answer is none.

As children, boys and girls are conditioned for their future. Girls are often told to go to college, get married, and have kids. Boys are often told to go to college, get a good-paying job to provide for their future family, get married, and have kids. This has been the norm for years. As the years pass there has been an increase in people not following that norm though. Men and women are both deciding to not go to college, to not get married, to not have children, and to choose a path less traveled.

I am a woman who has chosen to go down a path less traveled. Coming to this decision was not easy though. Several different experiences, traumas, and opinions have encouraged me to come to the decision of not wanting children. I believe I was eighteen when I started to think about the possibility of not wanting kids. To be more specific it was about a month after my eighteenth birthday when I started to seriously think about it.

I was dating a guy, we will call Mike for the sake of his own privacy, my senior year of high school. We were involved and on my eighteenth birthday, the condom broke.

I took a pregnancy test about a month later and it came back positive. I stood at the bathroom sink with the test sitting on the counter and cried silently. So many thoughts and questions began swirling around in my head. "What am I going to do?" "What is my family going to think?" "What is Mike going to say?" "I'm going to lose my scholarship." "Can I even care for a child being a child still myself?" "Fuck."

I went to Mike's house that night and told him the news. The look on his face gave me the final answer that I needed - there was no way I was having that baby. I went to our local health department where they gave me a pregnancy test to confirm that I was pregnant, gave me pamphlets with the options that I had, and sent me on my way. Because of our situation, we decided that the easiest way to terminate the pregnancy would be through the Abortion Pill. Thankfully we were able to order the pills online and have them shipped directly to his house to maintain our own privacy. With a Medicated Abortion, you can take the pills in your own home and you do not have to have a medical procedure done. We were trying to keep it as private as possible because we did not want outsiders stepping in and trying to make decisions for us.

We received the pills in the mail a few days later and I began the process. When you decide to do a medical abortion there are not one, but two pills you take: Mifepristone and Misoprostol. You take Mifepristone first and that will block the hormone progesterone, allowing the pregnancy to stop developing. Misoprostol is the second pill you take and this causes cramping and bleeding. You can take the second pill right away, or up to a few days after.

When I started bleeding I knew that the pills had worked and I experienced a couple of different feelings. The first one was relief and the second was grief. I didn't expect grief. I laid in bed and cried. I cried for hours. The cramping I was experiencing was nothing compared to the menstrual cramps I would get. Through the tears, my thoughts swirled, but one thought I kept coming back to was, "Do I even want children?" This was the first time I questioned it. The first time I really thought about what having a child meant to me. And at that time I couldn't come up with many reasons besides a feeling I had over and over - fear. The fear of not being able to provide for a child. The fear of not being able to protect them. The fear of not being a good mother. The fear of not being able to give them the childhood I wish that I had.

After the pregnancy was terminated I went on with my life as if it never even happened. I went to school, I went to work, hung out with friends, and tried to forget about it. I didn't tell anybody about the abortion, not for a long time. Mike and I were the only ones who knew about it.

I understand that everyone will have their own opinion on this. I know that some people would have decided to have that baby and either keep it or give it up for adoption. And that would have been their decision to make. If I could do it over again I believe that I would have made the same choice for myself. There are a few things I would have changed about the way I approached it though. I would have gone the proper route as far as doctor appointments go. You should have one before an abortion takes place and after. Both of which I did not do. This is a safety precaution for you and should not be ignored.

I also would have reached out for a bigger support system. When I was 18 I felt very alone for a number of reasons. I was not in the best mental space and I did not feel like I could trust many people with this decision. Knowing what I know now at twenty-six I would've reached out to certain family members and friends. I would have talked about it more instead of holding so much in until now. To my friends and family who are learning about this now, or have learned about it recently - I'm sorry. I'm sorry I didn't come to you and trust you when I now know I could have. Please know you did nothing wrong as to why I did not share this part of my life with you then. I was young, naive, scared, and extremely lost.

If you are ever faced with this decision please reach out to your support system. You will need them through the transition. If you know someone that is going through this or has gone through it either support them or don't say anything at all. This decision is already hard enough to make. And if you don't feel like you have that support system, reach out to me. I will be your support system. I will be your rock.

~ ~ ~

Transitioning into adulthood I always had the idea of kids in the back of my mind and the never-ending question of whether I wanted them or not. And as time went on I began to realize more and more that I was leaning towards not having them. I continued to have the argument with myself until one day I just decided that having kids was not in my life plan. By the time I made this decision, I was already in a committed, long-term relationship. I knew that I had to talk to him about the subject to make sure we were both on the same page.

I have been with my partner, Justin, for eight years now. It has probably been about four since we had the children discussion. I remember talking about it and we both agreed that children were not in our game plan at that time. We also agreed that once I turned twenty-eight we would revisit the topic and that it was my choice since I would be the one going through the pregnancy. Knowing that Justin is on the same page as me and having him make it clear that it is my choice has made so many things in our relationship and lives that much easier. With my twenty-eighth birthday quickly approaching, I still remain firm on my decision to not have children. And I can confidently say that my partner is okay with that.

As time goes by we still think about the child aspect of our life. It is very easy to get caught up in the "what ifs." Justin and I will often times say things like "If we were to ever have children we would raise them this way" or "If we have kids I hope they have [insert specific physical feature here.]" Although we have these moments, we continue to talk about reasons to not have children.

Justin and I have both accomplished many things in the eight years of being together. One of our biggest accomplishments, I think, would be moving out of our home state, Illinois, to East Tennessee. With our initial move, we had plans to stay in East Tennessee, but life had other adventures for us. Within six months of moving Justin was offered a traveling position that landed him in North Carolina. Soon we both found ourselves packing up our apartment and cats and heading further East. About a year after this move, Justin's traveling ended and we bought a home back in Tennessee.

We both have many dreams and goals we still want to fulfill. We both talk about having our own businesses one day. We talk about traveling all the time and the places/things we want to experience together.

I know people will say, "Well you can do all of that if you have kids." And they are right, you can. You can move out of state while having children. You can start a business while having children. You can travel while having children. But it would make things a lot harder and let's be honest - life is already hard enough as it is.

Neither of us thinks that this world is or is going to be one that we would want to raise a child in. The cost of living right now is ridiculous. I have friends and family who have children and when they tell me how much they are spending I truly do not know how they are making it. Some days I feel like Justin and I are barely making it by. And we are only two people. I can't imagine what families of 3, 4, 5, 6+ are going through.

Although there are several reasons we do not want children as a united front I can't forget to look at myself and my own personal reasons why I do not want children. I have reached a point in my life where I am truly happy. I am finally starting to heal and come to terms with aspects of my past. I enjoy the quiet of my surroundings, my freedom, and my independence. But I still do not know who I am fully yet. I am still learning to love and take care of my mind, body, and soul. Throwing a child into the mix wouldn't be beneficial to either of us.

I do not want to put my body through the physical changes/traumas that come along with pregnancy and the birthing process; morning sickness, aches/pains, swollen breasts, tearing, the possibility of shitting myself during birth, etc. I have put my body through enough as it is by my own hand. I believe she deserves some rest.

I'm scared. That fear that I felt at eighteen has followed me into adulthood, but I have more fears now than I did back then. The fear of not being able to provide for a child. The fear of not being able to protect them. The fear of not being a good mother. The fear of not being able to give them the childhood I wish that I had. The fear of losing a child - before or after the birthing process. The fear of losing my patience. The fear of losing my freedom. The fear of losing all the progress I have made as a person. Some of you may not understand these fears. Some of you may think they are ridiculous. And some of you may think that I will never get over these fears unless I have a child and that is something I can not get on board with. To me, it is not worth the risk.

~ ~ ~

When Justin and I started telling people we did not want kids we were met, and are still met, with a mix of responses. "You guys would be great parents." "It's okay to not want kids." "I just don't understand why someone wouldn't want kids." "It's your choice." "You're still young. You can change your mind." And my personal favorites - "You're selfish." "I will pray for you to get pregnant." Some responses are hard to ignore, especially when some come from your own family. I try to not address them, but there are a few I would like to address now.

**"You're selfish."** I don't think I am selfish for not wanting kids. I think it would be more selfish of me to have a child knowing I do not want them. **"I will pray for you to get pregnant."** Please don't.

~ ~ ~

From my past to my present to my future, I do not see my decision to not have children change. I can't tell you for sure what the future is going to look like, but I can tell you how I envision it. I see myself sitting on a covered front porch with Justin overlooking a lake, or a mountain range, sipping on coffee and enjoying our surroundings. I see myself tending to a garden and picking fresh veggies and fruit that we grew ourselves; maybe we will have a small farm and I'm tending to chickens. I see myself sitting in a comfortable chair reading one of the hundreds of books off my to-be-read list, or maybe even writing a new book. I see myself watching *Harry Potter* for the hundredth time. I see peace and freedom. The one thing I do not see are children, and that is okay.

## Shannon Jefferson

Founder of Majik Mentality

heal.me/bewise
www.facebook.com/majikmentality
www.instagram.com/majikmentality

Hey family!

My name is Shannon and I am a healer. Being a healer is my calling and birth rite. I guide people on their healing journey through Reiki healing, channeling, basic herbal remedies, and sound healing. As a wife and mother of five children, I know the struggle of back burner syndrome! The horrible habit of putting our needs LAST, resulting in a pile of anxiety, depression, brain fog, and despair. I look forward to helping people remember their Majik by prioritizing self-care and self-love. We deserve to be our best selves. I'm here to make the ride a little less bumpy.

# SHATTERED-MY HEALING JOURNEY THROUGH PPD

By Shannon Jefferson

I watched my baby boy struggle to breathe as the water in the tub surrounded him. His tiny body was flailing while the water splashed and I heard the sound of a rapid heartbeat blaring in my head. Suddenly he stops, he's still, with vacant eyes staring back at me under the water. A shrill cry, with massive force, snatches me out of my mind and into reality. My son is alive, in our bedroom, crying out for me. But I dare not touch him. Standing in our bathroom, I can't allow him to look at me with those eyes. Anguish overcomes me as I cry too. I don't deserve him, or else these intrusive, soul-shattering thoughts wouldn't be. The vision of harming my precious baby should not be. I love him. I look at myself in the mirror and whisper, "What's wrong with me?"

These intrusive thoughts, along with depression and anxiety, are the symptoms that manifested during my battle with Postpartum Depression for the first time. I have given birth to five children. With each birth, I endured PPD symptoms in various forms, all of which were as soul-snatching as the first. With my second birth, this sickness became evident through blackouts, extreme

mood swings, resentment towards my baby, and constant personality comparisons to my firstborn. After my third child, my eldest daughter, the PPD signs were the most unsettling. I could feel my psyche shift into different mannerisms and speech. I would have dissociative episodes where I would talk and act like a child. At least, this was what my family informed me of. The mood swings would go from high to low in a matter of seconds, with the faintest whispers of suicide. By my fourth birth, I thought I was an expert, but I had so many bouts of blacked-out sadness I barely remember our connection. The fifth and final birth, during the COVID-19 pandemic, came at such a cost, that my spirit demanded I cease the idea of procreating ever again.

Episodes of forgetting who and where I was, daily anxiety-induced seizures, and dropping out of college were all I could bear to sacrifice. Something had to give!! Therapy and medication were not enough. I absolutely had to heal myself. After a suicide attempt by the lake with my husband's gun, my Spirit Guides submersed my vision into an epiphany. I was launched into a place of a spectator, watching my life line go by. The feelings were raw, but I have names for them now. Contempt, sorrow, obsession, separation, self-loathing, and peace. The peace only connected with the sights and sounds of my children exiting my being and entering once again while being thrust upon my chest. The courage to not pull the trigger rests with Spirit and Spirit alone because in that moment my will to live was refreshed and I became whole. But the lingering dread of the aftermath of each birth still fermented in my gut. According to society's programming, having a baby should be a joyous time for all human beings and their families. So why was I so riddled with pain? Why was my soul slammed into so much darkness during what was supposed to be the happiest time of my existence as a woman?

With each birth, I reached out for help. I found support in my family, group therapy, talk therapy, Dialectical Behavioral Therapy, and the Child Protective Services System in Green Bay, WI. If you tell a doctor that you have thoughts of harming your child, they have to believe you and react accordingly. I was hospitalized and medicated after birthing my two eldest children. Both inpatient admissions were voluntary, but the medications made me feel like a zombie and even more disconnected. With each new pregnancy, I was abruptly taken off of their psychotropic cocktails and became a literal, raging maniac. I loved my children but these emotions were too much for two people to triumph. Once I was taken off of medications during my third pregnancy, I decided to never use them again. Instead, my Guides honored my heart by showing me that self-love and self-care were my most reliable allies.

As I walked through my journey to heal, I took notice of some crucial points that explained the reasons for my symptoms. When I stayed in the sacrificing spirit of society's requirements for motherhood, I became weak, suicidal, aloof, and bitter. I also noticed that when I used psychotropic medications to combat my symptoms, I became timid, a sleeping giant, detached from myself, and horribly unpredictable. I was also sick from withdrawal symptoms every time I was taken off of the pills during pregnancy, just to have them suggest taking them while breastfeeding. I questioned the doctors about my baby's hardships once I decided to wean them, but they weren't too concerned. I felt so unsure. I was afraid of myself and the mistakes this illness could lead to. A particularly challenging experience with my eldest daughter, third birth, diminished any further doubts I had about medicating going forward.

One night, I was all alone with my newborn baby. My husband was at work, and the baby wouldn't stop crying. Sadness took over my mind, so I started to pray. I begged God to give me strength. "Please Spirit, tell me what to do," I cried. I looked into my daughter's eyes and I realized her cry was not the call of Motherhood, but the wailing of the child within myself. My inner child who yearned for validation, love, attention, and a voice. So I answered by allowing my heart to fully connect to this inner child through the love I gave my baby, without the blockage of psychotropic medications. This decision worked for me. Other women may come to a different conclusion for their unique situation. Keeping ourselves present, safe, and sane is the top priority and psychotropic medications are a tool to do so. I would encourage everyone to do their research, talk to their doctor, and do what's best for them. As for me, medication became a double-edged sword. My mood swings were less frequent, I smiled more, and had fewer instances of suicidal ideation. On the other hand, if I missed a dose or became immune to the dosage, my symptoms came back in full force. My low points were so devastating that I couldn't fight the urge to cut myself, hit myself, isolate, or destroy my house in a fit of rage. My happiness didn't feel genuine but more like a button being pressed in my brain to make me laugh, smile or stop crying. I felt even more numb towards my children and family. Most days, I would just exist in a haze, high on Xanax and mood stabilizers. No thank you!

As mothers we may question, "Was this a mistake? How did I let myself go? Where is the person I used to be?" In reality, we have always remained present, just transformed. We sacrifice our bodies, our minds, and our beautiful souls just to forsake the sacrifices that lead to our own existence. The Majik of it all wasted away in dirty diapers, a sink full of dishes, and sleepless nights. I know my power and I honor my mother's sacrifice by adopting the Majik Mentality. I honor my willingness to give up my Trinity (body, mind, soul), with daily self-care practices, self-love, holistic remedies, and self-acceptance. I don't have to live up to society's standards of what a mother should or shouldn't be. I no longer greet this God-given gift with the cookie-cutter view of harmony and happiness but with tact and the guttural awareness of this unique transition. I've managed to make Majik Mentality my way of life through various forms of clinical therapy, research, and spiritual practices. The first and most important practice is giving myself grace. I practice talking to myself the way I would talk to a friend. I look for reasons to be proud of myself and compound these reasons by saying them in the mirror. I use herbal remedies as medicine as much as possible to reconnect me with natural healing from the earth. I hug trees, forage for food, sunbathe, and do water meditation. Getting out in nature is surprisingly the most potent elixir a human can take. I pray and practice gratitude daily. The key to all of this being so effective is that I engage in these activities even when I feel depressed. It's painful, but the more I do it, the less sad I feel. It's Majik!

Over 70%, or 1 in 7 women, will experience PPD after giving birth, and 20% of them don't make it out alive. I have survived the storm of such a sacred position five times. I am here to allow other selfless women the space, and the opportunity to heal from this life-changing masterpiece called Motherhood. Mental illness, postpartum depression, and postpartum psychosis exist, but so does Majik Mentality. This is a call to all mothers. Remember your Majik, Mama Bear! And if you forget, I am the evidence of triumph and victory. It's fair to put yourself first. Your babies and inner child will thank you for it.

# REDEFINING DIVORCE:
# FROM DESPERATE HOUSEWIFE TO BADASS MATRIARCH

By Jennifer Williams

Divorce: the ultimate suck fest. And throwing kids into the mix? Suck level: off the charts!

None of us enter marriage expecting it to end like this, but somehow, half of us end up in the divorce boat. Even when we know there's no hope for a fix, the whole process of divorce is a nightmare. It drains us financially, mentally, physically, and emotionally. And let's not forget about our poor kids, stuck in the middle of our mess with no say in the matter. It's a life-altering experience for the whole family, even our furry friends. But guess what? It doesn't have to stay that way.

Divorce brings a hurricane of emotions, uncertainties, and changes. It's a tough journey that can leave us feeling like we've lost our way. But here's the thing: life is all about change. We've got to embrace it, grow from it, and tackle it head-on. As women, we have the power to empower ourselves, let go of our fear of the unknown, and embrace change with style and resilience.

Here's my story…

## Setting Boundaries: The Harsh Truth

In September of 2017, Hurricane Irma barreled across my home state of Florida. It was an extremely stressful time for Floridians causing millions to evacuate, leaving behind severe damage, and leaving millions without power for weeks, my family being one of them.

That's when my life changed. I was unexpectedly entering a new chapter in my life which I had been expecting and avoiding for years.

After our return, it felt like we were inside a sweltering sauna within the walls of our home. Our family of five found refuge in the master bedroom, the only room in the house with a window AC unit powered by a small generator.

The turning point occurred when my husband, having spent the entire afternoon drinking with his subordinates completely missed dinner with me and our children. We had planned to dine at his mother's, the only place with a working oven that we knew of.

He returned home hours later in an intoxicated state, appearing utterly unaware of our ongoing disputes about his dangerous drinking habits and the fear it instilled in me.

His alcohol-laden breath and the vacant look in his eyes, as though he were peering right through me, filled me with nothing but contempt and disgust. It became glaringly evident that this time, the customary peace offerings of flowers the next day could no longer conceal the deep wounds. My patience had reached its breaking point, worn down by his consistent disregard for our well-being.

Strangely, I didn't react immediately. I was seething with anger, yet strangely composed, almost chillingly so.

After three days of silence, he sought a conversation. We sat on the back porch away from the children, gazing at the serene river by the gentle flicker of candlelight. He pleaded and attempted to rationalize his actions.

Amidst the mayhem of toppled power lines, uprooted trees, and a chorus of gas generators humming in the background, stood an eerie stillness.

It was then that a resounding, clear voice inside me declared, "he's never going to change." I turned to him and, when he inquired if I intended to leave him; a pang of fear in his eyes, I replied with a simple "Yes."

Six weeks later I was living in my new home, navigating joint custody, and looking for divorce attorneys.

If you change nothing, nothing will change.

## In Retrospect

In the rearview mirror of my life, my failed marriage is now a distant chapter, one filled with painful lessons, introspection, and ultimately, gratitude.

As the marriage approached its inevitable end, the legalities of our divorce further exposed the rift that had formed.

A postnuptial agreement, cleverly worded and presented under duress years prior after discovering his affair, cunningly eliminated the alimony and minimized the financial support that I was entitled to after investing 25 years into that relationship. I was left with minimal severance, a fraction of what I should have received. It was a cold, calculated move on his part, one to keep me from leaving him and punish me if I did. It opened my eyes to the harsh reality that I married an asshole.

As the dust settled and the divorce became a part of my past, I learned that sometimes the end of a relationship can be a new beginning. It's a chance to rediscover oneself, to reevaluate what truly matters, and to pursue a life that aligns with personal values and aspirations. My failed marriage, despite its challenges and heartache, ultimately provided me with valuable insights and the opportunity to grow into the person I was meant to be.

Navigating change can be daunting and unsettling. When my marriage ended, it felt like my entire world was thrown into chaos, leaving me feeling lost and stripped of my identity. Suddenly, I went from being a dedicated spouse and full-time stay-at-home mom to a divorced part-time mom, trying to find my way through the uncharted waters of co-parenting. I felt like I had no purpose and battled with the overwhelming fear of an uncertain future and facing judgment from others. The fear of being alone loomed over me. While I knew deep down that ending my marriage was the right decision, the speed at which everything was happening was overwhelming and terrifying.

Embracing change also requires a willingness to step outside of your comfort zone. It may involve venturing into unfamiliar territory, trying new things, and taking risks. You may find yourself moving into a new house, looking for a new job, taking on responsibilities your partner once provided and even dating again. While change can be intimidating, it is often the catalyst for personal growth and transformation. By embracing change and letting go of resistance, you challenge yourself to discover new strengths and capabilities. This, in turn, builds resilience and empowers you to navigate the challenges of single motherhood with confidence.

Six years later, these are the lessons I have learned thus far.

## Locus of Control

One of the key skills I adopted is understanding my locus of control. It's the degree to which people feel in control of their lives, and it can be categorized as either internal or external. When we have an internal locus of control, we believe that our actions and decisions have a direct influence on the outcomes of our lives. On the other hand, when we have an external locus of control, we believe that outside forces such as luck, fate, or other people are the predominant factors.

Traffic is external - we can't control whether there is traffic or not. However, our reaction to the traffic is internal - we can choose what we do while we are stuck in it.

Another example of external factors is other people. We can't control other people despite the illusion we sometimes trick ourselves into believing. We are not responsible for the thoughts, mindsets, actions, or feelings of others. But we can control our reactions towards them and our own mindset.

Understanding and focusing on our locus of control allows us to let go of the things we cannot control and focus on the things we can, bringing peace and happiness.

I had no power over my husband's actions, no matter how much we fought about them or how hard I tried to change him. It was beyond my control and he made his choices. The decision to leave was within my grasp and it shaped the person I am today and gave me the best gift of all.....an independent life without him.

## Forgive Them. Forgive You.

By adopting an internal locus of control, you shift the power from external circumstances to your own actions and choices. And in doing so, you create a pathway that leads to forgiveness – not just of your ex, but of anyone who has ever hurt you...especially YOURSELF.

Have you ever held onto a grudge for too long, unable to move on from a past hurt? It's a heavy burden to bear, carrying that anger and resentment within you day after day.

As a divorced mom, thriving has become one of my greatest priorities. It may seem daunting, but forgiving my ex-husband has allowed me to be authentically happy and a true super-mom.

At first, forgiving him felt impossible. But as I started my journey of healing, I realized that holding onto anger and resentment was only hurting myself. It's scientifically proven it is cancerous to our health, mental and physical.

Finding forgiveness was a difficult journey for me. I had to let go of the bitterness towards him, even without receiving an apology or any acknowledgment. It was tough, but I realized that his actions were a reflection of his own struggles and inner demons. He used money as a weapon, causing pain in our shared history of 25 years and three children. Despite his justifications, I now understand that I deserve inner peace. I choose to send him positive vibes, whether he deserves them or not because I believe in radical self-acceptance.

As I look back on my journey, I've come to realize the mistakes I made not only as a spouse but as a flawed human being. I am far from perfect, and I know I will make more mistakes in the future because that's what humans do. There were mistakes I made in my marriage that my ex-husband could possibly forgive me for, but I also needed to learn to forgive myself. It's a realization that often goes unnoticed by many of us.

Forgiving is not just a one-time act, but a continuous choice to make every day. I realized that each time I chose to forgive, I grew stronger - both as a person and as a mother to my children.

## Honoring the Blended Family

As a single parent in a blended family dynamic, I believe that honoring the roles of all parties is essential to thriving. Even though it may be difficult at times, I hold myself accountable for displaying respectful behavior towards my ex's new partner.

It's not about me liking or agreeing with her, but rather it's about acknowledging the significance of her role in my children's lives. Ultimately, I choose to put my grievances aside, recognizing that the happiness of my children is the ultimate goal.

This practice has become one of my values and strengths. Sometimes, it may feel like taking the high road is a lonely journey, but in the end, it is always worthwhile. I encourage others in the same situation to embrace the blended family dynamic with grace and understanding.

It may not always be easy, but it is always necessary for the well-being of our children. And in the end, it's ultimately easier to get along than to carry the weight of anger and hostility.

## Invest in Yourself

Taking care of yourself is not just about taking a break or indulging in pleasures. It's also about investing in your future and personal growth.

For me, this meant going back to school to pursue a career in a field I was passionate about as well as participating in intense therapy and discovering the power of life coaching.

Though it was challenging and time-consuming, it was fulfilling and meaningful. Investing in myself improved my career prospects and modeled to my children the importance of education, personal growth, and self-discovery.

After my divorce, I undertook a transformative journey, engaging in years of therapy, life coaching, and personal development. These experiences were instrumental in breaking free from a victim mentality and embracing my post-divorce life. Therapy and coaching equipped me with the tools to navigate the emotional challenges of divorce and find personal empowerment and self-discovery. I finally found myself and discovered my life's purpose.

## Build a Support System

Cultivating resilience hinges on the strength of your support network. Surround yourself with individuals who comprehend and stand by you, cultivating a profound sense of belonging and empowerment. Engaging in conversations with those who've confronted analogous challenges can furnish you with advice, motivation, and affirmation. Keep in mind, that you're never alone; your support system is there to offer both emotional and practical aid when it's needed the most.

It really does take a village.

## Getting My Groove Back

Following my divorce, I was hesitant to re-enter the dating scene. I was concerned that it would hinder my ability to focus on my personal growth and my children. It felt strange because it had been over two decades since I last navigated a new relationship. However, I knew that I deserved and desired a fulfilling romantic connection.

I soon learned that dating was more than just finding a partner; it was a journey of self-discovery and understanding my boundaries and desires. This experience gave me a newfound sense of control and authority, becoming an act of self-care, and allowing me to prioritize my happiness and love life while still being an amazing mother to my children.

Taking risks and plunging back into the dating world boosted my confidence. It was a powerful reminder that I still had my groove and that everything was going to be alright.

## Final Thoughts

In the journey of redefining divorce and transitioning from a desperate housewife to a Badass Matriarch, it's crucial to keep in mind that change and resilience are your greatest allies. As a single parent, you have the power to reshape the narrative of your family and to define success on your terms. Striving for balance is not only a possibility but a path to thriving in your role.

Undoubtedly, there will be tough days and daunting decisions ahead, but it's essential to remind yourself that you are more than capable, and this belief can be a game-changer. Your strength serves as an inspiration to your family, and safeguarding your physical, mental, emotional, and financial well-being is pivotal for achieving all your goals. Embrace each obstacle with confidence, seeing it as an opportunity for growth rather than succumbing to fear or self-doubt.

In this redefined chapter of your life, challenges are not burdens but exciting adventures that ultimately lead to success. So, don't back down from them; instead, embrace them with open arms, knowing that they are stepping stones towards a future filled with triumph and newfound purpose. Remember, you are the architect of your destiny, and in this redefined journey, you're not just surviving – you're thriving as a Badass Matriarch.

# PART 4:
# Breaking the Silence

In this deeply personal and introspective section, we embrace the courage to confront the often unspoken challenges that many women encounter on their life journeys. With unwavering empathy, we acknowledge the profound strength and resilience that arises from overcoming these hurdles. Within these pages, we dare to shatter the suffocating silence surrounding critical topics like birthing trauma, grief after losing a child, and the intricate complexities of widowhood.

Here, we celebrate the triumphs of survivors, the unwavering spirit of advocates, and the faithful support of compassionate souls. Together, we provide a sanctuary of understanding, validating each woman's unique experiences and nurturing the seeds of empowerment that blossom in the face of adversity.

## Prudence Todd

Founder of Your Womanhood

www.facebook.com/prudence.todd.5
www.instagram.com/yourwomanhood/
Free Facebook Support Group
www.facebook.com/groups/healafterbirthtrauma

Prudence Todd is the Founder of Your Womanhood and is deeply passionate about women's experience of womanhood, birth, and beyond.

As a previous Midwife and now Holistic Pelvic Wellness Practitioner and Restorative Pilates Instructor, Prudence helps women heal their hearts and body after birth with her online and in-person healing sessions. She specializes in guiding women to reconnect with their bodies, access their intuitive wisdom and medicine within, and in turn heal pelvic floor trauma and dysfunction.

Prudence believes our womanhood is the portal to so much that rests within us and that birth and pelvic floor dysfunction call us home to address these issues.

Prudence creates safe spaces for women to talk about the impact of Motherhood and their birthing journeys.

When she's not helping women heal, Prudence loves walking the beach, swimming in oceans and creeks, and experiencing the joy of her loved ones and life itself.

# HEALING THE HEART AND BODY
# AFTER BIRTH TRAUMA.

By Prudence Todd

*If you are reading this, I want you to know it is such an honor to share with you what is resting in my heart. Thank you for being here and thank you for what you have gifted to the world just by being you.*

*I share these words here with you from my heart, from the place of being 'with woman' and witnessing the process of women healing after birth, and the strength and surrender that takes. I speak with words of love, encouragement, and truth according to the way I see the world and the women around me in it.*

To every woman I speak with who has birthed a baby, I ask the question, "Sweet Woman, how are your heart and body feeling?"

I ask this because, in my experience with guiding women to heal after birth, I've learned that we simply cannot separate the heart and the body. Both the emotional and the physical impact of birth on our body are so deeply profound and both call to us in different, yet interconnected ways. The emotional and the physical are inextricably interwoven and both have to be cared for in order for true healing to happen.

Yet rarely is this common phenomenon spoken about, especially when women have experienced birth trauma.

So, as you find yourself here reading this, Sweet Woman, I ask you, "How are your heart and body feeling today?"

Since the birth of your babe or babes, what rests deep within you that calls to you within the quiet moments of your day? Does it show up as a deep sigh? A nagging thought? A pain in your back, your belly, your womb? Or perhaps a deep ache in your heart?

So many women I speak with feel broken, disconnected, and ashamed, and carry guilt through their experiences of birth. Some of them wonder if their experiences even 'justify' the love and care required to heal.

I am here to tell you there is NO woman who doesn't qualify for the love, care, and listening it takes to heal after birth. You are worthy of this, Sweet One. Your story and experiences are real and valid!

## What is Birth Trauma and Have I Experienced It?

So perhaps you're wondering, how do I know if I have experienced birth trauma?

Birth trauma is subjective and varies from person to person. It's not something that someone else can say you did or did not experience, as it's personal to each and every one. We know that 1 in 3 women experience birth trauma*. This is a huge portion of women, who go on to become mothers and raise families, journeying along with this trauma as part of their life experience. For many weeks, months, and sometimes years after giving birth, many women feel there is nowhere to go and/or no one to listen who truly understands what they have been through. This can leave a mother feeling isolated, numb, anxious, disconnected, and unable to reach out at a time of life when she most needs community, connection, and loving support.

I wonder, how has your experience impacted you as a woman, a mother, and a partner? Has the death of your dream birth resulted in you feeling like a stranger in your own body?

If you have experienced feeling physically and/or emotionally wounded or mistreated you may feel the impact of these wounds resting in your body. As a Mumma, we tend to go on in life with such deep love, distracted from these places within us that need to be healed. Our devotion to loving this new little human we brought into the world captivates our hearts. What I have witnessed in my experience caring for women is that these wounds can manifest as deep, emotional scars and then deepen into ongoing physical symptoms (often within the pelvis). More often than not these symptoms emerge as the heaviness rests deeper into the heart and body unaddressed.

So why do these experiences become trapped and held in our bodies?

The cells of your body are witness to every experience you go through. Cells will carry the memories with a charged emotion attached to them. This charged emotion subconsciously impacts your life and alters your ability to connect deeply with your body and experience the joy of motherhood you desire.

For harmony and healing to return to the body it requires a safe process of holding your reality and listening to how it truly deeply impacted you. When you feel safe, the underlying grief and trauma of your body start to tenderly emerge to be healed.

## How Do I Begin to Heal?

As a previous Midwife, Restorative Pilates Instructor, and now a Holistic Pelvic Wellness Practitioner, witnessing women heal and come home in their bodies after birth has taught me so much about how women carry trauma in their bodies and how this impacts the body physically. The emotional trauma a woman feels can sometimes lead to physical pelvic symptoms and other times the physical pelvic trauma can lead to emotional heartache. They are deeply interwoven.

For some women, this heaviness and ache in the body may be carried for years, and only discovered and healed many years later. For others, the physical impact of birth on their body can be so painful that trauma from their life previously is immediately triggered. These feelings in one's body are calling for love and attention. This, Dear One, is where we start; wherever the body feels safe to begin and is requesting your love and care.

## Emotional Impacts

The way we experience trauma in our bodies is unique to all of us. Mostly, however, when I speak with women, some of the common themes that come up are as follows:

Why didn't my body work for me?
I feel ashamed that my body wasn't able to birth well.

I don't feel connected to my baby. I let my baby down.
I feel so unheard and angry.
I didn't feel like I had a voice.

My wishes weren't honored.
I don't know what went wrong.
I feel guilty for wanting a different birth when I know many other women have had worse.

My story isn't as bad as others. I should be happy.
I had a beautiful vaginal / home birth – why do I feel unhappy?
I feel so ripped off and angry.
I felt so alone – unheard – unseen.
I don't enjoy intimacy anymore.
I feel disconnected from my partner. Numb. Guilty for not wanting sex.
I feel like I've let my baby down because I couldn't make enough breastmilk.
My heart aches.
I wake up with flashbacks in the night.
I relive and rewrite the story over and over in my mind.
I am constantly feeling like something is going to happen to my baby.

And so many more.

When we look at how women suffer physically after a traumatic birth, we also find shame arises because these things are not 'okay' to talk about. Normally, as long as the baby is well and the mum looks fine, everyone assumes the Mumma is ok.... but many of us know this is not the case. Here are but a few of the physical impacts women talk to me about.

## Physical Impacts

Painful vaginal scarring and/ or infection.
Leaking pee or poop.
Constipation. Hemorrhoids. Prolapse.
Aching tailbone – not being able to sit comfortably for weeks or months.

Pain in the pubic bone.

Aching pelvis.
Scar pain. Numbness. Not wanting to be touched. Aching Vulva.
Rectal pain.
Lower back pain.
Upper back pain.
Heartache.
Fatigue, depression and anxiety.

Many of these symptoms can be layered and complex, and require a combination of emotional release, tender nurturing and holding, and the gentle application of aware breathwork and conscious body movement in order to heal. Through compassionately listening to what your body is asking for, you can heal the suffering resting in your body from your birth experience.

## Compassionate Healing

So, I ask you, Sweet Woman, "What is your body asking for?"

Are you feeling estranged from who you are as a woman? Vacant in your body, disconnected from your baby, or distant from your lover? Perhaps you aren't even sure how to articulate how your life and world have changed or how you feel since the birth of your baby.

The impact of a traumatic birth can be far-reaching and also very subtle at the same time. Some of the words I hear women say are:

- 'I felt completely violated'
- 'I wasn't given a choice'
- 'I prepared so much only to be let down by my body and those around me'
- 'Will I ever be able to have a beautiful birth?'
- 'I have never felt the same since my birth/ miscarriage/ abortion'
- 'I feel numb and completely overwhelmed'
- 'I don't feel connected with my baby'

All of these 'feelings' are your body calling to you. So how do we tend to her and help her to heal?

One of the most powerful methods of healing your body from trauma is developing the skill of compassionate listening and dialogue with your own heart, mind, and body. Just as you communicate with your children or partner with compassion, your body craves to be listened to with deep love and compassion. As you begin this journey, your body starts to soften, and the 'stories' of what you have experienced start to emerge and you can listen in more deeply. Trust starts to build over time and I have witnessed huge shifts, softening, and release for Mummas through the simplest of communications done with love, tenderness, and compassion.

## Try This Exercise Now

Find a quiet place to sit or lie down. Take a few deep breaths, slowly exhale, and allow your heart and mind to be still. When you feel ready, gently, either out loud or in your mind (whatever feels more connecting for you) speak these words softly…

"I'm here, and I care." Pause and listen.

Feel what sensations awake or reveal themselves within you. Perhaps there's a simple relief and tears start to flow, perhaps you feel the need to ask more…

"How are you feeling today?"

This dialogue, seemingly so simple, is so powerful in allowing your body to feel safe. I invite you to try this every day for a week and just see how it shifts things within you.

Perhaps as you start to check in, feelings of anger, rage, or disgust start to rise. Uncomfortable feelings and sensations that cause us to feel uncertain and scared can begin to 'open up', unveiling themselves for healing. If you find this happens, be patient, and love these sensations in your body. Sit with them and allow the words to flow again in love to your own heart and body.

"I'm here and I care."

Say it over three times, slowly, thoughtfully, and lovingly.

## Healing Pain vs Suffering

One of the blessings in disguise I am so deeply grateful for in my journey as a woman and a mother is learning how to decipher suffering and pain in my body.

This became clear to me after the death of my brother five years ago.

My brother's death, so very sudden, left me in shock. My body was wracked with pain both physically and emotionally. My depression I had healed, returned as anxiety, a constant worry about the future. It was debilitating to the point where in spite of all of my efforts of 'trying' to do the 'right thing', I wasn't getting better. One morning, three years after my brother's death, my husband took me to the emergency ward to find support. This was the beginning of yet another road to healing for me, after already deeply suffering from postnatal depression twice within my 10-year period of birthing babes. My depression had led to me feeling incredibly sensitive and incapable as a mother, always questioning my choices and whether I was enough. After healing this (more on this in the last chapter of this book), I was devastated to find myself amid total disarray and despair, slowly turning inward once again to find just the tiniest piece of strength to start over.

I began to take notice of how, when, and where sensations showed up in my body. I combined noticing these feelings with stillness practice, deep compassionate listening, breath work, and body movement. As I gently tended to my body with love and care, I started to notice the suffering I was feeling in my body lessened. The pain didn't just 'go away', but it began to ease and transform as I lovingly followed my body's cues. The more I loved her, the less she suffered and the louder I received messages to guide me towards what she needed to take care of the pain.

Quite often I would find it was something so very simple. When I 'checked in' and was still and quiet she would say, "Make a cup of tea", "Go to bed early"', "Take the afternoon to watch the sunset", "Sit and breathe in your bedroom on your own for five mins", "Take a breath." Sometimes the requests were so simple that it was hard to justify the follow-through, but this, Dear One, is where the healing magic and medicine really are.

Sometimes the request would require me to ask for support or for someone to step in for me so I could take time for myself. I would easily justify to myself that it wasn't 'worth it', but this, Dear One, is again where the healing magic and medicine are.

So, I ask you, how do you deal with the pain, Sweet Woman? What are you feeling? Is it calling to you? Are you able to tune in; do you need support?

If so, I truly see you in this and encourage you to reach out. So often I find the *thought* of the healing process is sometimes more painful and complex than the healing process itself.

When guiding women to heal, many of them will say to me, "You know that really simple thing you asked me to do? Well when I started doing it, it really worked!"

It's in the little things, Sweet Woman. The lessening of distractions from the pain. The quietness to hear your soul speak truth. It's the tuning in that brings awareness to know what she is asking of you to heal. When we build this relationship of love with ourselves we learn how to carry the experiences we have been through and then go on to draw wisdom and strength from them (read the last chapter of the book for more on this).

Your willingness to surrender to this will bring ease like when your close friend holds you in a deep hug and your body softens.

It's there for you to access, Sweet Woman.

If you need deeper support you can connect with me via my FB community page www.facebook.com/groups/healafterbirthtrauma/

Or linktree linktr.ee/prudencetodd

xx

## Kaitlin Jackson

My name is Kaitlin. I grew up in northern Illinois. I have one son who is my guardian angel, and hopefully one day he will have some siblings on Earth. My favorite hobby is traveling. It's on my bucket list to make it to all 50 states in the US. At the time of writing this, I have been to 30 states. I have a Bachelor's Degree in Biology. I love science and animals. I can't pick my number one favorite animal, so my top three favorite animals are sharks, elephants, and jaguars. All sharks are cool, but my favorite shark is the Black Tip Reef Shark. I also enjoy watching sports. One of my favorite summer hobbies is attending Major League Baseball games. My favorite hobby in the fall is watching football games. I'm amazed by sunsets, oceans, and mountains. Life is hard, but it is worth it.

# MY GUARDIAN ANGEL

## By Kaitlin Jackson

Honestly, I don't know if I could ever fully move on. Maybe about 90%, but I don't know if 100% is achievable. I have conversations and laugh with my friends, family, and favorite colleagues. I go about my workday like usual. My husband and I have date night on Fridays to kick off our weekends. We play with the dogs and take care of the chickens. For most of the time life is normal. But then, I hear a song on the radio, and the singer is talking about his beautiful, pregnant wife. Or I hear a baby cry while I'm at the grocery store or one by one, I find out several of my colleagues are pregnant. Of course, I'm happy for them, and I put on a brave face. When I find myself alone, it cuts me like a knife. The pain in the center of my chest is so crippling I can't swallow. I can't breathe. I give a single thought about my angel, and instantly, the tears well up in my eyes. I can't say his name. I can't go into his room that's still decorated for his arrival. I get frustrated when my family brings up the subject. I know this is selfish because everyone is grieving too. Our parent's grandson is not here. My brothers' nephew is not here. My husband's son is not here, but I just can't talk about it.

I would give anything to be able to go back to my last prenatal appointment. It was a Tuesday. I got to hear his heartbeat, and the doctor asked me, "Are you ready to have a baby?" "Yes" is the only word I could think of to say. But I was beyond ready. I was so excited to have my son in my arms and to be his mommy. I was so excited to have my husband by my side as I went through the most difficult, but the most rewarding moments of my life. Before leaving the clinic, we scheduled me to be induced the following evening. I called my supervisor at work to let them know I was officially going on maternity leave. I told my husband to inform his supervisor as well. I told my mother, who was in town for the special occasion, to prepare herself. We were at the final countdown.

Finally approaching my last few hours of pregnancy, I was 39 weeks and 3 days pregnant, and I could hardly wait. I was to the point of being physically miserable. My belly was so big it hurt. My lower back hurt. My pelvis hurt. It hurt to stand or sit. I hadn't slept in my own bed for weeks because I couldn't get comfortable anymore. Instead, I resorted to the recliner in the nursery. My wrists and ankles were swollen. My wedding ring no longer fit my ring finger. The index and middle fingers on both of my hands were numb from the swelling. All of these things were normal but incredibly uncomfortable.

I patiently waited for the last few hours to tick away. My husband and I got the car seat secured in the truck. I finished up the last of the baby laundry. My mother and I did some last-minute cleaning. At one point in the afternoon, I remember thinking that I hadn't felt him move around for a while but being busy, I figured that I just hadn't noticed it. We were going to be at the hospital in a couple of hours, everything should be fine. Finally, the time came to head to the hospital. After arriving and checking in, we waited for our turn to be called back. There was another couple that walked in just a few moments before us. They had so much stuff. Two suitcases, blankets, pillows, and a car seat. I started doubting that we brought enough. We had two duffle bags and a backpack. Eventually, our nurse called my name, and we headed to our suite. She got me hooked up to the monitors, and I heard his heartbeat again. I felt a little relieved that my little guy was hanging in there with us. The nurse asked me all the medical questions, and I figured we would be getting going soon. Then, she tells me that he isn't moving. The feeling in the room changed. It went from anxiously excited, to concerned. The nurse suggested a C-section. My heart broke a little, but I quickly agreed. Anything I needed to do.

Very quickly, my son's healthy heartbeat started dropping. I could see it with my own eyes. 120 down to 100 beats per minute. The nurse told me to lie on my side. As soon as I did, his heartbeat dropped to

90. I'm watching my son die and I can't do anything about it. Suddenly, everyone was in a panic, and I was whisked away to the operating room. My mom had a look of terror on her face as we left. "2222," the nurse called out as we entered the OR. "10:22pm" I thought to myself as the bright OR lights shined in my eyes. The nurse instructed me to slide onto the operating table. Next thing I know, I'm naked from the chest down. The blue drape was hung. The doctor started applying iodine to my lower abdomen. It burned. I was cold. I was scared. The anesthesiologist told me that I would feel a burning in my arm, and that was just the anesthetic. Just as he finished saying that I could feel the burning, and then I started dreaming. I was dreaming of being in a huge field of flowers. I was alone. I was trying to find my way back home, but I couldn't figure it out. Why couldn't I find my way home?

The bright lights came back. I blinked my eyes realizing I was awake again. "Where's my son?" I struggled to speak. I realized I had been intubated. I had never been intubated, under anesthesia, nor had surgery before. My throat hurt, and I kept coughing when I tried speaking.

"He's in the nursery," someone said to me. "Everything must be fine then. He's in the nursery." I thought to myself as I was being wheeled back to the room. The nurse pushed on my abdomen, and I felt like I was dying. The pain was so immense, I had never felt anything like that before. Suddenly, my mom appears by my head.

"Oh, Kaitlin, he's so beautiful!" My mom cried to me. I felt a little jealous that she got to see him before me. Then, my husband appears. He's holding my hand and hugging my head. Then the nurse pushes on my abdomen again. I nearly broke my husband's hand, but I didn't even realize I was grasping it that hard. The pain was so surreal.

"Where's Cade?" I asked my husband.

"He's in the nursery, but he's intubated. They had to do CPR, and he must go to the Children's Hospital." He keeps explaining to me that our son is in fact not doing well. The realization started setting in. "The ambulance is on its way to get him, but he's beating the breathing machine." My husband kept explaining. The nursing staff hurriedly had us sign a few papers. One of them reads his time of birth. 10:43pm. I was staring at this paper when the emergency staff came into the room with my son. They let me get a look at him before they had to rush off. All I could see was an incubator with a bunch of wires and tubes. I could see his arm. I strained to get a good look with groggy eyes, but the emergency staff said they needed to get going. All I could do was nod my head. My husband made the difficult decision to go with them. He didn't want to leave me behind, but he also didn't want to leave our son. I told him to go. After they left, my mother also left the hospital. We had been at the hospital for many hours, and she needed to take care of the dogs. She kissed my head and left.

I was alone. The occasional hospital staff checked every hour or so. I was so exhausted, but I couldn't let myself fall asleep. My husband was texting me letting me know they arrived at the Children's Hospital. He was explaining to me how exhausted he was too. I told him it was okay to sleep. Eventually, we both gave in. A few hours later we finally had the opportunity to speak over the phone. Our son had acid in his blood, the brain scan wasn't showing any activity, his kidneys were not functioning, and he had suffered a lot of injuries. The epinephrine they had him hooked up to was the only thing keeping his heart beating now. My college education was not in healthcare, but I had the understanding that he was not going to survive. I asked the children's doctor about his prognosis anyway. She told me what I already knew. Speaking to my husband again I said with a breaking heart, "We can't let him suffer. Steven, we can't let him suffer." My husband didn't have many words, but he agreed. The doctor spoke up again, I didn't realize she was still listening.

"If I'm hearing you correctly, you want him taken off life support?" She asked in confirmation.

"Yes," I told her.

The next couple of hours were spent figuring out how we could be reunited before he died. One of the other doctors offered to give me a ride in her personal car, and our game plan was in motion. I mustered all the strength I had to stand. The pain again was so immense, it took my breath away. I stood there for several minutes, as I wrapped my head around the pain. The nurse stood by my side as I willed my legs to move. Very slowly, but surely, I made it to the bathroom. The nurse helped me put my clothes on. My doctor pleaded with me to make sure I took care of myself while I was away. I appreciated her concerns, but I had to make it to my son. Finally, we were on our way. The drive was only 20 minutes, but it took so long to get there. The doctor driving attempted to make small talk, but I couldn't even focus on what she was saying. As we arrived at the Children's Hospital, I thanked her for her graciousness.

I was taken to my son's room in a wheelchair. When I arrived, I was greeted by my father-in-law who was already sobbing. I was wheeled to the side of my son's bed. Finally, I got to see his face. "So beautiful," I thought to myself as I pulled myself to stand. I grabbed his little hand. His skin was so soft. He was still hooked up to all the machines. As reality sunk in again, my husband held me in his embrace. We stared at our dying son together. My mother arrived at the Children's Hospital and shared that my father was on his way. He was seven hours away, and I was so nervous that he wouldn't make it in time. The Children's Hospital staff let me get comfortable again in my wheelchair and pulled a recliner next to me so my husband could sit. My son was then placed in my arms. He was so heavy; I could barely hold him. Several pillows were placed under my arms to support his weight. I just stared at him. Not long after, we finally decided to take him off all life support. For four hours, he made his final gasps. Everyone took turns holding him. I held him as his life faded. His skin went from pink to gray. His eyes no longer sparkled. I tried so hard to keep him warm, but I couldn't. His final gasps sounded like cries. I kept wishing that he would come back to me. One final gasp, and I knew it was finally over. At 6:24pm the hospital doctor confirmed his heart had finally quit beating. My father arrived a few moments later. Although my son had officially passed away, my dad held him, and I felt some relief that he at least got to meet him.

We scheduled his funeral for the following week so my parents, who live out of town, could be there too. One by one, our closest friends, family, and work colleagues come to pay their condolences. I take one last look at my angel, realizing I will never see him again, and then we set off for the cemetery. His tiny white casket was buried and covered in flowers.

Months after his passing, my state of sadness was so heavy; I wished someone in a passing car would crash into me during my commute so I could die too. I got so drunk, I held cosmetic scissors to my wrist, but I couldn't make them cut me. I didn't have the desire to eat. I truly felt there was no reason to keep living, but I didn't have the courage to take my own life. I was stuck in my misery. We spent the following year figuring out how to pick up the pieces. Many others shared their similar experiences and reassured us that everything would be fine. Each day my husband and I took small steps together. We have slowly found ways to laugh again. We have found ways to enjoy life again. Slowly, daily life gets easier to bear. We've gone back to our normal routines. We keep our son's picture on our dresser. I'm so relieved that I can always remember what he looked like. I wear a necklace with his name around my neck. My surgery wounds have healed, and my heart is a little less broken. One day at a time, we rebuild our strength to keep moving on. There are times when we are still sad, but we find comfort in the fact that he is not suffering. He will always be innocent and never have to experience how harsh this world is. One day we will be together again, but for now, we know that we have our guardian angel always watching over us.

## Krystal Casey

Flight of the Phoenix Collective
Women's Empowerment Coach

www.krystalcasey.com
www.flightofthephoenixcollective.com
www.facebook.com/flightofthephoenixpage
www.instagram.com/flightofthephoenixcollective/

A resilient widow and mother of five, Krystal Casey is the force behind Flight of the Phoenix: A Women's Empowerment Collective. Rising from unimaginable tragedy, she's an international best-selling author and a powerhouse motivational speaker dedicated to breaking generational cycles of trauma and sexual abuse.

Beyond her advocacy, Krystal finds solace in the tranquility of the beach, revels in the magic of live music, and thrives on the thrill of exploring new places. Whether orchestrating the chaos of family life, shattering societal stigmas, or indulging in her passion for true crime docuseries, Krystal embodies the multifaceted nature of strength and resilience. Her story serves as a testament to overcoming challenges, and she harnesses its power to ignite a fire within other mothers. Krystal empowers moms to rediscover their own spark, step into their power, and create a life they truly love living.

# EMBERS OF INTIMACY: REIGNITING LOVE & PASSION IN WIDOWHOOD

By Krystal Casey

"Til death do us part."

You don't realize the gravity of those words until you're fulfilling the vow.

Widowhood, a word that holds so much weight, is a journey you never imagine you'll have to take as a young bride. It's not something you can prepare for, even if you do see it coming. And there's no telling just how hard the grief is going to hit, how long it will last, or how it will affect who you become.

## The End of Forever

When I lost my husband as a young mom of five, my world was shattered. Not only was I blindsided by his sudden, unexpected death, but I was sucker-punched in the gut having discovered the dark and twisted hidden life that ultimately led to it. The sting of his betrayal ran deep, puddling into pools of resentment and anger, which eventually bubbled into impermeable walls.

I found myself grappling with a void that seemed insurmountable. He had been my heart's love since I was 12, and the idea of ever regaining that deep emotional bond with anyone else felt impossible, not to mention the last thing I wanted. The trauma surrounding my loss further eroded my trust in others, leaving me questioning my ability to love, let alone be loved once more.

Unlike many of the widows I've met in the past few years, my marriage was troubled, and it had been for years - in ways I couldn't even see at the time. Unraveling the truth caused me to question everything about myself: my worthiness, my sexiness, my character… down to the very essence of my womanhood.

And just as the embers of self-pity cooled, a new flame sparked - something I later learned is coined "widow's fire": an intense, all-consuming desire for sex following the loss of a partner. In other words, you start to *crave* sex! This unspoken phenomenon is something that happens to be quite common among widows.

But I had never heard of it before, so the intensity of this newfound longing both surprised and overwhelmed me. However, after some research I realized that this yearning for intimacy was not something to be ashamed of; it was a natural and valid part of my grieving process and it deserved attention.

As I dove deeper into this wave of emotions, I also recognized the importance of honoring my feelings without acting on them impulsively. I knew that for me seeking physical connections solely to fill the void left by my late partner wouldn't truly heal my heart. Instead, I chose to embrace the concepts of self-intimacy and self-love, recognizing that my worth and healing did not depend on external validation.

## From Self-Love to New Love

Through a summer of self-exploration, I discovered the power of nurturing a profound connection with myself. Though the widow's fire burned brightly within me, I recognized that this powerful energy could be directed toward rediscovering my identity beyond the confines of widowhood.

Who am I now, if not his wife?
What did I want, if not the life we had been creating?
Where was I going to go from here and what was I going to create now?

Instead of seeking intimacy externally, I channeled this fire toward reigniting the spark of self-love within me. I embarked on a journey of self-discovery, exploring what brought me pleasure, joy, and fulfillment.

This process allowed me to connect with my desires on a deeper level, enhancing my capacity for intimacy and emotional bonds.

Widowhood offers you the opportunity to reevaluate your connections and redefine what intimacy means. Through this process, you'll discover that intimacy isn't confined to the romantic realm; it extends far beyond, touching every aspect of your life.

Self-intimacy means getting to know, accept, and love the various aspects of who you are. It's exploring your inner world, getting honest about what you find, and loving it enough to allow your authentic self to shine. It's being mindful of your energy, your boundaries, and your connections, while trusting your judgment in these areas, knowing your worth.

And when you dive in and peel back these layers to reveal, empower, and cherish yourself for who you are, romance may just appear when you least expect it - as it did for me.

I didn't know it was romance at first. In fact, it wasn't. It was the opposite, actually. When he, my late husband's best friend, reached out to me after the tragedy that shattered my world, I was initially hesitant to engage with him. The trauma surrounding the loss of my husband made me wary of connecting with anyone from his circle. I had built emotional walls around myself, and he was one of the last people I wanted to speak to during that vulnerable time. I told him so, too.

To my surprise, he responded with genuine compassion and empathy. Unlike others who had remained silent about the trauma or defended his best friend, this man chose a different path.

He said he understood.

He acknowledged our experience. He respected my feelings, and most importantly, he asked about my kids and how he could help support them.

At that moment, I felt seen and understood in a way that I hadn't experienced since my husband's passing. He shared in my sorrow and disbelief, offering unwavering support and companionship during those dark days. From that point on, he has been walking with me on this journey of healing.

Initially, our relationship was grounded in friendship. We got to know one another as he stepped into the role of a true friend, doing all the things friends do when you need them the most. He took me out to divert my mind from the pain, binge-watched TV shows with me, provided me with a safe space to cry, vent, or process the different aspects of grieving, and always provided a comforting shoulder to lean on. He was a pillar of strength both for me and for my kids, ensuring they felt seen, loved, and supported unconditionally.

As time passed and emotional intimacy grew, the lines of friendship began to blur almost imperceptibly. It wasn't a sudden realization, but rather a gradual understanding of the deep connection we had formed. I recognized how much he had been there for me, offering unwavering love and support without any expectations. I began to understand how I wanted to be loved, appreciated, and valued in a relationship - and that it was a stark contrast to the compromises and settling I had experienced in my marriage.

The sparks of affection that I thought were long extinguished within me began to flicker again, a testament to the resilience of the human heart and its capacity to heal and open up to new possibilities. The possibility of romance with him felt unexpected, weird even, yet incredibly genuine. It was a revelation that love could find its way back into my life, and I could embrace it with a newfound understanding of my worth.

The road from friendship to romance was one of self-discovery and empowerment. It taught me that love, in its purest form, should uplift and inspire us to be the best versions of ourselves. I realized that I deserved to be cherished and adored for who I am, without having to settle for anything less. With him, I found the courage to be vulnerable again, to trust in the strength of my heart, and to embrace the joy of connection.

Through the blur of friendship and romance, I found the love I never knew I was capable of experiencing once more. It was a love that grew from the ashes of grief and loss, defying all expectations and filling my heart with hope. Our relationship has become a testament to the resilience of the human spirit, showing that love can find us when we least expect it and guide us to a future filled with love, connection, and healing.

While new love can never replace my last one, it has been a profound catalyst in my healing journey, igniting a spark within me that I thought was distinguished forever. With this love, I have discovered the ability to create a life filled with passion and pleasure once again, and it has been nothing short of transformative.

## Fueling the Fire: Physical Intimacy

One of the most valuable lessons I learned from my previous relationship was the significance of intimacy - specifically, what happens when it fades. Physical intimacy plays a crucial role in nurturing a deep and meaningful connection between a couple. It goes hand in hand with emotional intimacy and is an essential aspect of bonding on a profound level. The power of touch, affection, and closeness cannot be underestimated, as they create a unique and irreplaceable sense of unity between two people. Lack of physical intimacy will erode the emotional intimacy - it's just a matter of time.

And I'm not just talking about sex (though that is important, too).

Physical intimacy is about more than just the act of lovemaking; it includes all forms of physical affection and closeness, from holding hands and hugging to cuddling and kissing to simply being present in the same space at the same time. These acts of physical connection are not only pleasurable but also release oxytocin, often referred to as the "love hormone" which fosters feelings of trust and bonding between partners.

Moreover, physical intimacy creates a strong foundation for emotional intimacy to thrive. When we feel desired and connected on a physical level, we become more open and receptive to emotional vulnerability, fostering a deeper emotional bond between partners.

Not to mention that getting close can reduce stress and improve overall well-being! Physical intimacy has been scientifically proven to reduce stress hormones like cortisol, promoting a sense of relaxation and contentment. Sharing physical touch with your partner can offer comfort during challenging times and remind you that you are not alone in navigating life's ups and downs.

This is why my partner and I are intentional in making these connections. When we engage in physical intimacy, we become more attuned to each other's needs and desires. Whether it's getting creative together, participating in a new experience, or snuggling up to our favorite show, we're building a safe space where we both can feel accepted and cherished. In these moments of physical closeness, we're able to communicate our affection and care without needing to say a word.

In this process, I've also come to appreciate the importance of play and fun in both our relationship and life in general. Engaging in playful activities together fosters a sense of joy, lightness, and camaraderie that strengthens our bond, while laughter has become the secret ingredient to sustaining it.

Whether it's sharing a meal at our favorite restaurant, playfully bantering during a game night, or creating new memories on random adventures, we prioritize moments of play and fun. It adds a touch of magic to our relationship and reminds us not to take ourselves too seriously.

After all, we know all too well just how precious our time here together is.

## When is the Right Time to Love Again?

Only you can tell.

It's essential to recognize that physical intimacy can be deeply personal and varies from one person to another. What matters most is finding a comfortable balance and pace that aligns with both your and your partner's needs and desires. Keep communication open and honest when it comes to your preferences, boundaries, and consent to ensure that physical intimacy is a mutually fulfilling and enjoyable experience for you both.

In the context of widowhood and navigating new relationships, physical intimacy can represent a transformative journey. It can be an opportunity to rediscover your sensuality, connect with your body, and embrace the joy and pleasure that intimacy can bring. By approaching physical intimacy with an open heart, vulnerability, and respect for your unique journey, it becomes a powerful aspect of healing and growth after loss.

Applying this newfound insight to my current relationship, I have witnessed the growth of a love that burns strong, slow, and constant. We are intentional in nurturing our emotional and physical intimacy, cherishing the moments we spend together like tending to a fire that warms our souls and keeps us close, even during the coldest of times.

Rediscovering love and the importance of intimacy, I've come to understand that healing isn't about erasing the past or replacing what's been lost. Instead, it's about embracing the full spectrum of your experiences, revealing your authentic needs and desires, and allowing your heart to open to new possibilities.

I've learned that love can find its way back into your life even when you think all that remains in you are ashes. And when you approach this new love with intention, vulnerability, and a commitment to self-discovery, it can grow into something remarkable, allowing you to cherish the past while embracing the future with an open heart.

## Carrying the Torch

One of the greatest lessons I've learned through my loss is the healing power of sharing my story. Now, I'm on a mission to help other moms who have experienced trauma or tragedy and are feeling unseen, unheard, or unfulfilled to rediscover their voice, their vision, and their passion. The journey from feeling stuck and overwhelmed to stepping into a space of empowerment is nothing short of awe-inspiring and I'm proud to light the way.

As an Empowerment Coach, I share valuable insights and tools to help women embrace their sensual selves, which is a vital aspect of self-intimacy. In *From Stuck to Unstoppable*, a virtual course I created featuring 36 expert lessons, we guide you through the same 6 steps I used to reignite my own spark after becoming a widow. This transformative resource equips moms with the guidance and support they need to reclaim their power and reignite their inner spark. It's about discovering the magic within and creating from the limitless potential that resides within each of us.

There is no "right" way to grieve, no timeline for when we should open our hearts to new emotional connections. Our journeys are unique, and we must honor our individual paths. But even in the face of loss, the flame of love within us never truly fades; it burns eternal, lighting our way to a future filled with love, connection, and healing.

As widows, we are not defined by our loss, but by our strength to rise from the ashes of grief. This includes reconnecting with ourselves and embracing the warmth of newfound intimacy when we're ready. It takes courage and vulnerability to put ourselves out there again, to take that leap of faith into the unknown. But as we do so, we discover the beauty of human connection and the resilience of the human spirit. Though our paths may be unique, the flame of love within us never truly fades. Through vulnerability and self-love, we can once again ignite the fires of passion and pleasure in our lives.

# PART 5:
# Navigating Life Transitions

In this transformative section, we stand at the crossroads of various life passages, ready to embrace the transitions that shape us. As we venture into adulthood, we confront the beauty and challenges of becoming a woman, navigating the uncharted waters of responsibility and independence. Together, we unveil the power of empowering conversations, guiding the next generation towards a healthy understanding of intimacy - with self, with others, and even with money.

As time weaves its intricate tapestry, we approach the profound phase of menopause, ready to reclaim our vitality and rediscover our inner strength. With candor and compassion, we engage in open dialogues about the changes, both physical and emotional, that redefine our womanhood.

Here we find the support and resources needed to traverse these life-altering moments with grace and confidence. So, let's embark on this final leg of our journey, hand in hand, as we embrace life's transitions with resilience, wisdom, and an unwavering spirit.

**Lauren Carpenter**

www.facebook.com/profile.php?id=100042972578315
www.instagram.com/_mystical.gaia_/
www.instagram.com/mystical.sage.777

Lauren is a college student and the eldest of six children. She has always had an affinity for natural elements, along with both people and animals of all kinds. As a child, swimming in her grandparents' pool and digging in the dirt were her favorite pastimes. Her love for nature and connectivity only grew stronger, morphing into her desire to become a naturopathic physician and cultural anthropologist of folklore and medicine. As the eldest sibling, and an avid empath, connecting to people and understanding their livelihood through actively engaging with them offered an attractive opportunity for Lauren's future. Combining her quest for global knowledge and understanding with the spiritual sensibility of plants, animals, and the world around her, she aspires to travel the globe and interact with people who have stories to share and lessons to learn while learning and providing natural remedies. Follow my Instagram to share my journey!

# TRAVERSING WOMANHOOD

By Lauren Carpenter

As a product of military parents who divorced, my visions of being an adult were about what I longed for to be true in my own life. Ideally, I wanted my parents to be together and live happily ever after. I thought being an adult meant being with someone forever - that's all.

Marry rich! Marry someone well off - that's what I was told. But I don't want to marry for money, I want to marry for love. If they don't have money then I'll be the one to make it. I always saw myself living on a large plot of land with an abundance of trees and animals, throwing in a few four-wheelers and maybe some kids. Worrying only about happiness and love and nothing else. Having enough money to be comfortable but not so much that you never knew what to do with it. Not having to worry about bills and the ability to just live carefree.

Since my parents were divorced, I primarily lived with my mother. I have been fortunate enough to be surrounded by many other strong women as well. I watched as my mom, aunts, grandmothers, and great-grandmother lived their lives, seeing all these women in different lights and taking on different roles. To be a woman meant being bold but not too bold. Being pretty and smart but not too much as to outshine others, including men. Growing up I thought that I didn't want to be a"suzy-homemaker", yet I also wanted to be able to whip up a delicious meal and feed my loved ones with pleasure. Rosie the Riveter mixed with a little Betty Page- be strong and able to handle yourself while being a femme fatale.

"Princess," this was the one thing I never wanted to be. I loathed when people would call me that as a little girl, and I never aspired to be one as an adult. But isn't that what little girls are supposed to dream of? The norm for little girls is to grow into the adult version of prom queens. That was not my dream and seemed highly illogical to me even as a young girl. However, it raises the question of how being an adult and being a grown woman intertwine. Society tells young ladies to be strong, fierce, independent, and take care of themselves. Yet, society also tells us to be safe with the "buddy system" when going out and that safety can be found with a strong man. So, to be safe with someone else but also be independent seems contradictory despite societal views. It doesn't have to be that way. It shouldn't be that way. I was and still am determined to NOT be that way without risking my safety or independence. I've learned how to stand up for myself from a young age and take no shit from anyone. I'm willing to throw down if I need to thanks to growing up with a former active marine father and several siblings- think Family Feud meets MMA.

My stepmother has always said, "It's your life, you are the one that has to live it." Whenever I am faced with choices, unsure of which to make, this quote resonates in my mind to remind me to do what makes me happy first and foremost. What I do and the consequences that follow are mine and mine alone to deal with. As women, we are tasked with choices every day that can impact our futures. Simple things like the clothes we wear and how we appear to the world on any given day- to open ourselves up with communication and learn to grow as life progresses. My wise uncle once told me, "Don't hold yourself back from anyone, you are more than capable," and while I know that I am, at times my own anxiety creeps in and scares me into backing down from opportunities. It's in those moments, when my anxiety is winning on the battlefield, that I hear my Nana and Granddaddy. Nana's warm, loving, and tender voice wraps my mind in a gentle hug and Granddaddy's light-hearted, soft, southern twang envelopes me in safety and comfort. As some of my biggest cheerleaders growing up, they always told me how smart, kind, and gracious I was. Maybe as my great-grandparents they were biased, but I felt I could do anything with them supporting me. Even when I felt defeated, their words lifted me from the depths of depression and allowed me to reach for the strength I often forgot I had. As I sit here in tears, thinking of the dreaded day when they are no longer with us, I'm reminded of how much their love and words have molded many fibers that are my being. While it is sorrowful, I'll forever be grateful to the universe for sending me such wonderful people.

At 16, I met a wonderful and charming young man and we clicked in ways that I never thought were possible. We talked about our pasts, our dreams, and our futures, and I could actually picture my life with this man. It was at this time that I realized that I wanted to think about someone else's happiness and future just as much as my own. Our newfound relationship was eye-opening for both of us. Neither of us had felt this kind of connection and love before and it was in this moment we wove our dreams together. While I had my own demons and past sexual anguish that put sex into a dissociative category, he woke up something inside me. I gave him my purity, and he gave me a connection and insight into what love could really feel like. We hadn't been together a full year yet when my mother hit me with the plans to move almost three hours away. I found love and now it was moments away from being torn from my arms, how is that fair? We put our heads together and tried to come up with solutions for how we could stay together. We could move into an apartment, but we were still in high school, so how would we work and make enough money to support ourselves while finishing school? Our minds were flooded with possibilities that, once we talked out, were just not feasible. Our hearts ached with the thought of losing what we had just found. An opportunity arose - to move from Texas to Illinois and live with my father, stepmother, and younger siblings while they allowed us to finish high school and set us up for the future we had been dreaming of.

This was not an easy decision as I had lived in Texas with my mother most of my life. I was extremely close with her side of the family and was worried that being so far away would have me miss out on so much. To say my Poppie (grandfather) was not a fan of this plan is probably the understatement of the century. While it is my life and I felt this was an adult decision, I was told I was being childish and too young to understand what love really was. Full-blown screaming matches ensued. Even though I had a plan well thought out and would be in the safety of my family, they struggled to accept my choices. Meanwhile, my other half's side chose to stay silent and cut off communication with him, all the while picking up the phone to call me every name imaginable. Still, we persisted and leaned into each other for support.

At this point, the advice started pouring in. I've been told to "Be a sponge and soak it all in, " and that's what I did. Listening to words of advice from everyone who could get a hold of me, I took it all in and weighed my choices. It's MY life and I'm not going to hold myself back from what is going to make me happy. This was not the first nor last time I was given life advice I didn't take. Be a lady, be ladylike - what does that even mean? I am a lady, but I'm my own definition of a lady. I am my own woman. I am an adult and I am making an adult choice to live with the person who makes my heart happy.

While advice often comes in the form of criticism, it can be very difficult to learn to read between the lines and find the lessons that are trying to be conveyed. It always comes from a good place with good intentions, but when that lesson isn't clear and bold it can be very easy to miss. This leads to learning lessons the hard way, firsthand with the pain and embarrassment to boot. The universe has such a funny way of teaching lessons over and over until you learn them, and they get harder to withstand every single time. I learned sending pictures wasn't as innocent as I imagined, and got burned when that picture was forwarded to multiple people. When scandal is involved, things tend to spread like wildfire, scorching your ego and leaving your self-consciousness exposed in its ashes.

While trying to maintain my strong and independent image, anxiety and depression festered underneath. I had always tried to come across as this tough, self-reliant person but under it all, there was pain that yearned to be released. My release: self-harm. It started off slow, with little cuts here and there; over time it gained more power over me until it went fully up my arms and onto my legs. My family knew and tried to help by allowing me to explore other outlets to release my pain. It was never enough to extinguish it though. It finally hit me that what I was doing was not healthy and not how my stress should be handled. That blow came in the form of the love of my life when I saw that my release was causing him to question his worth in my life and ask if he was the cause of my pain. I knew then that it had to end. I couldn't bear to see something I did cause someone else so much pain and angst. He held me accountable for my actions, which, for an independent person, is probably the most difficult task I've ever had to face. I leaned into communicating; I allowed myself to open up and convey when I felt pain. I had to learn to get comfortable being in an uncomfortable state in order to heal. I had to be open when all I wanted to do was shut down and release. I still think about the release from time to time. However, I chose to listen to my inner voices of strength and lean into my support to persevere.

As I grew into adulthood, I realized that while society may say how I should act and attempt to dictate my future, I am the one in control. Just as my decision to move across the country with my partner that I love showed me how to adjust to what lessons life threw at me, he opened my eyes to more opportunities on how to best overcome adversity in becoming my own person. Our decision to live together, despite the odds being against us, gave me the confidence to pursue my dreams without fear of ramifications and instead focus on the improvement our opportunities can offer. Our world isn't always safe and learning to defend myself has been imperative for my well-being and survival. Believe it or not, the buddy system is not a hindrance to independence and shouldn't be viewed as a lack of autonomy. It's a form of accountability that allows you to be in control of your own safety and aid another person's as well. Over the years I have learned that it is important to always be willing to learn while being humble and be willing to observe and adapt to whatever life throws your way. If ever given the choice to be right or to be kind, always be kind because the world needs more kindness.

Although I still have plenty of adulting left in my future, I'm working every day to push myself forward. I've had my fair share of setbacks but it's not stopping me. As I continue to traverse the complex terrain of womanhood and adulthood, I've come to understand that life is a journey of constant self-discovery. The lessons learned along the way have reshaped my perceptions, challenged societal expectations, and strengthened my resolve to be true to myself.

I've defied stereotypes and norms, refusing to conform to anyone else's idea of what I should be. I've embraced my own unique blend of strength, independence, and femininity, knowing that it's the authenticity of who I am that truly matters.

One of the most valuable lessons I've learned is the importance of taking control of my life. My stepmother's words, "It's your life, you are the one that has to live it," resonate in my mind, reminding me that my happiness should be a guiding force in my choices. I've realized that it's not selfish to prioritize my own well-being and aspirations.

Through the hardships and mistakes I've faced, I've come to understand that life's toughest lessons often come the hard way. But each challenge has been an opportunity for growth, a chance to learn, and a stepping stone toward becoming a stronger, more resilient version of myself.

As I look to the future, I am determined to push myself forward. I'm working and pursuing my dreams, striving to become a naturopathic physician and journalist so I can offer people alternative ways to heal both physically and spiritually. I dream of traveling the world, exploring cultural anthropology through folklore and herbology, and sharing the beauty of nature from diverse perspectives. And I know my dreams are within reach.

So, to all of you who may be in a similar space, remember this: Life is a journey of self-discovery and continuous self-improvement. Embrace your unique path, take control of your choices, and learn from your experiences. As you work towards your meaningful goals, don't be discouraged by the challenges you face. Instead, view them as opportunities for growth, and let them shape you into the best version of yourself. This is your life, and you have the power to make it a remarkable, authentic, and fulfilling journey.

# GETTING INTIMATE ABOUT FINANCES AS A WOMAN

By Brandi Liberty

In the intricate tapestry of women's empowerment, financial literacy stands out as a potent thread. For far too long, women have been sidelined or marginalized when it comes to money matters, often due to deeply entrenched societal norms and historical inequalities. But the world is evolving. More women than ever are realizing that financial empowerment is inextricably linked with personal and collective empowerment. By valuing themselves and understanding money matters, women can reclaim control, secure their futures, and chart the course of their dreams.

## The Genesis of Financial Intimacy

Before diving into the nuts and bolts of financial literacy, it's crucial to address an underlying principle: self-worth. As a woman, understanding your worth transcends the monetary. It's about acknowledging your unique strengths, capabilities, and value in every aspect of life, be it personal, professional, or financial. When I was asked to write this chapter, imposter syndrome immediately set in. How was I, a single mother who still lives paycheck to paycheck while owning her own businesses, going to write about financial empowerment?

Historically, many cultures relegated women to roles where they were not primary decision-makers, especially concerning finances. As Native women, we see where colonialism shifted our matrilineal societies towards an implied male dominance over decision-making. Even today, remnants of these beliefs persist within our tribal communities, and it is expansive across the world and other cultures. As a result, many women feel apprehensive about taking charge of their money and valuing themselves. Recognizing that these beliefs are outdated and not a reflection of one's ability is the first step toward dismantling them. The foundation of self-worth is often built on knowledge. Understand that you, as a woman, have every right and ability to comprehend complex financial concepts just as any man does. Seeking financial education is not only an act of empowerment but also an act of self-love.

Just as I learned to heal and find my self-worth after narcissistic abuse, I had to rebuild my autonomy and economic independence as a result of the financial abuse I endured during that marriage. Financial abuse, a sinister form of domestic violence, strips the victim of their financial autonomy. More than just a play for monetary control, it digs deep, emotional scars, leaving feelings of fear, inadequacy, and a warped sense of self-worth in its wake. Emerging from such an experience and attempting to rebuild trust in personal or new relationships can feel like scaling a mountain.

It hasn't been an easy feat to get to where I am financially over the last 10 years. As I discussed in my previous chapter, I'm still learning to value myself. Certain situations make me question my worth, and my financial struggles have led to those thoughts. I am blessed to have parents who helped me ensure my children and I always had a roof over our heads, a good education, and a way to the means we needed to sustain ourselves. As I sit across the street from the church where I got married, the challenges I have gone through, the ebbs and flows of financial well-being and hardships, resonate in my memories. I walked out of a narcissistic marriage with 37 cents in my wallet, the other $35 taken unknowingly from my wallet that same morning by my ex because he needed gas to get to work. I had a garage sale the weekend before and stashed a few dollars away knowing that the day I needed to walk out was on the horizon. Within a couple of years, I was financially independent of him, foregoing child support and other financial obligations to ensure there was no amount of control left in his hands.

It was from there that my financial journey became a goal-setting list of tasks that I checked things off of, year after year. Initiating a journey into financial intimacy starts with understanding one's financial self. The financial self is an amalgamation of one's earnings, spending habits, debts, and savings. It is critical to maintain a ledger of incomes and expenditures, initiating a habit of regular financial self-audits to develop an insightful perspective on one's economic behaviors.

## Emotional Intelligence and Finance

An understated aspect of financial literacy is emotional intelligence. It involves understanding the emotional triggers that lead to impulsive buying or being frugal in a negative way while creating a disciplined approach to financial management. Developing a higher emotional intelligence fosters better decision-making and a harmonious relationship with money.

As I began my journey to financial independence, my parents helped me out a lot. I held a full-time job through most of college, so it was not that I didn't have my own earnings throughout my pre- and post-marriage days. However, another aspect of the financial abuse was not being allowed to hold regular employment during the marriage. I was already an entrepreneur, writing grants for my tribe as a side hustle while trying to maintain my identity during my marriage.

Finding permanent, full-time employment was at the top of my to-do list immediately upon leaving. Being back in the workforce was a priority for multiple reasons, especially to help me find my worth and value to society in the work I had longed to do. Thankfully, I had the support of my family, social service programs, and a tribal community who I went to work for to help me get there rather quickly. I learned that it is okay to use the programs available at the federal, state, local, and tribal levels to support yourself and your family. The struggle is real, and it is okay to ask for help.

## The Pillars of Financial Literacy

This is where the imposter syndrome comes into play. I'm not going to pretend I have it all together even after all these years of being financially independent. I work with tribal communities daily, preparing budgets, educating them on financial management and literacy, developing projects and programs on their behalf, and have barely skimmed the surface of doing those things to the same capacity for myself. However, I'm not without the knowledge and understanding of what it takes to have the foundation of financial literacy.

Budgeting stands as the cornerstone of financial intimacy. It entails delineating one's earnings into different spheres of expenditure and savings, fostering a disciplined approach to spending while facilitating savings for future needs and emergencies. Valuing one's self-worth as a woman transcends societal roles, external pressures, and monetary value. While many might associate financial management with a mere practical endeavor, learning to budget can be a profound journey of self-discovery and empowerment. For a woman, taking charge of her finances can mean asserting control over her future, understanding her true value, and not letting external factors dictate her self-worth. Budgeting serves as a reminder that one's value isn't determined by material possessions or the balance in a bank account. Instead, one learns to recognize personal strengths, ambitions, and the impact she has on her community and loved ones.

Investment is a vital pillar of financial literacy. It is not just about growing wealth but also understanding various investment vehicles like stocks, bonds, and mutual funds. Women should embrace the journey of learning the ropes of investment, encouraging proactive participation in wealth creation. In the complex world of investing, a woman's journey to navigate her finances becomes intrinsically linked to her sense of self-worth. As women break barriers across various sectors, they are increasingly taking the reins of their financial futures, dispelling the myth that investing is a predominantly male domain. Embracing the world of stocks, bonds, real estate, and other investment avenues, a woman reinforces her belief in her capabilities, wisdom, and foresight. The process of making informed investment decisions not only amplifies her financial acumen but also bolsters her confidence, reminding her of her worth beyond societal norms and expectations. The act of investing serves as a testament to a woman's belief in herself, her vision for the future, and her unwavering determination to harness the power of compound growth not just for wealth, but for the enrichment of her life's narrative.

Mastering personal finances, whether through budgeting or investing, empowers women to assert control over their futures and enhances their self-worth. By taking charge of their monetary resources, women not only demonstrate financial literacy but also cultivate a deeper sense of confidence and self-respect. This journey transcends mere financial gain, evolving into a statement of capability, vision, and self-belief, defying societal norms, and reshaping perceptions of value and strength.

## Financial Wellness and Empowerment

Creating a retirement plan and establishing an emergency fund are pivotal steps for women seeking financial wellness and empowerment. These financial strategies not only provide a safety net for unexpected expenses, reducing reliance on high-interest debts but also offer peace of mind by alleviating financial stress. By proactively planning for the long term, women can ensure they are prepared for life's later stages, especially given challenges like the gender pay gap and longer life expectancies. These measures foster a sense of independence and autonomy, enabling women to make choices aligned with their personal and professional aspirations.

The process of financial planning also boosts financial literacy, helping women navigate other economic decisions with confidence. Beyond personal security, these steps can pave the way for broader economic participation, such as starting businesses and contributing to community growth. Through such proactive planning, women can potentially build legacies for future generations while securing their own financial future.

It's often difficult to get to these stages, especially as a single mother raising children on her own. For myself, these two steps of financial wellness have had ebbs and flows. I've created the emergency cushion, to only exhaust it during the ups and downs of owning and growing a business. As a business owner, retirement planning is even tougher as it adds another level of administrative burden to your business planning. However, it's an important part of planning for your financial future.

## Entrepreneurship and Financial Literacy

For aspiring women entrepreneurs, financial literacy stands as a steadfast ally. Being a female entrepreneur not only paves the way for financial independence but also acts as a conduit for self-realization and empowerment. By navigating the intricate pathways of the business world, a woman learns to trust her instincts, value her ideas, and assert her place in often male-dominated spaces. The entrepreneurial journey, with its inherent challenges and rewards, provides myriad opportunities for her to discover her strengths, resilience, and unique capabilities. Moreover, as a woman achieves financial autonomy, she gains the means to make choices that reflect her personal and professional aspirations, further solidifying her sense of self-worth. This combination of economic empowerment and personal growth fosters a deeper understanding and appreciation of her intrinsic value in both the business sphere and broader society.

I never set out in life to be an entrepreneur; it wasn't part of the plan. I had worked for businesses in a W-2 role since I was old enough to hold a job. For many women, the role of being an entrepreneur is not thought of as a business choice when first starting; rather it starts by doing various things you're good at to make ends meet. For many of us, that turns into a full-time role, for others it continues as a way to leverage one's income.

It took approximately ten years of being an independent consultant to realize I was an entrepreneur. I began to identify myself as a business owner and founder but it would take another two years and expanding into four businesses later to feel comfortable with calling myself a Chief Executive Officer, or CEO. I had built an expertise and reputation in my field of work, but I did not value myself enough to appreciate the self-worth that title holds.

## Financial Education for the Next Generation

Creating a legacy of financial empowerment for the next generation of women demands a comprehensive and interconnected strategy. Central to this is prioritizing education, encompassing both financial literacy—from the basics of budgeting and investing to complex topics like entrepreneurship—and in-depth career counseling to ensure women understand their workplace value and know how to negotiate effectively. Successful women should be encouraged to adopt mentorship roles, fostering invaluable, intergenerational dialogues and offering practical advice, networking opportunities, and inspiration. Community initiatives can further bolster these efforts. By establishing women-focused financial organizations, platforms for resource sharing, and training programs, we can cultivate an environment of mutual support.

Entrepreneurship is another key avenue. With dedicated resources and training for aspiring female entrepreneurs and an emphasis on venture capital support for women-led startups, we can further financial independence. Integral to all of these is the importance of role modeling to our peer women and young girls. Celebrating diverse success stories in media and other public platforms can instill a belief in young women that they too can achieve financial success.

Finally, true empowerment requires an inclusive lens. Acknowledging and addressing the unique financial challenges faced by women across varied cultural, socio-economic, and geographical contexts ensures a more holistic and intersectional approach. By weaving these strategies together, we lay the foundation for a legacy that propels the next generation of women towards financial autonomy, confidence, and valuing themselves.

## Conclusion

In the intricate tapestry of financial literacy and empowerment, we witness the deep interplay between self-worth, societal norms, and economic autonomy. For many women, this journey, although rife with challenges, becomes a beacon of self-discovery, resilience, and emancipation. From historical impositions to present-day adversities, women have had to confront a myriad of barriers to assert their rightful place in the financial realm. The stories of women reclaiming their worth, like that of a single mother emerging from the clutches of financial abuse or the subtle transformation from an independent consultant to a self-acknowledged CEO, highlight the indomitable spirit of women and their capacity for change.

Financial intimacy is more than just understanding numbers; it's about intertwining emotional intelligence, historical context, and practical knowledge. Budgeting, investing, entrepreneurship, and financial education become not just tools, but symbols of transformation. They represent a woman's journey to rewrite her narrative, to shatter ceilings, and to plant seeds of wisdom for the generations to come.

As we close this chapter, it is imperative to remember that every woman, irrespective of her background, possesses the potential to master her financial destiny. It starts with a simple yet profound realization of one's self-worth, followed by the commitment to acquire the necessary knowledge and skills. By sharing experiences, offering mentorship, and fostering a culture of continuous learning, we can collectively pave the way for a future where every woman stands financially empowered, confident, and deeply connected to her intrinsic value.

## Stephanie Carpenter

Stephanie is a 911 dispatcher in Illinois. She is a daughter, mother and wife to an amazing blended family with four wonderful children. When she's not busy serving her community and keeping the public safe, she can usually be found in her garden or crocheting.

Prior to working in 911, she used to work in the medical field for a private ambulance company. She has always taken on the role of caretaker, whether it's for a complete stranger or her family. She's always willing to lend an ear, cook a meal and take care of those who may need it most.

Stephanie has dealt with various medical issues as a result of her past lack of knowledge and inexperience. While not an expert, she speaks from experience and is always willing to educate, especially for women and their bodies. Today, she can be found sharing her gifts at work and enjoying her family.

# NAVIGATING MENOPAUSE AND RECLAIMING VITALITY: NURTURING HEALTHY CONVERSATIONS

By Stephanie Carpenter

The idea of womanhood was something that I never thought applied to me. I never thought of myself as a strong, empowered, or sexy female even though I've grown up watching beautiful women all around me achieve success. I don't recall being sat down and taught things about what my body should do, how to dress it, or make myself feel beautiful. To say my journey into womanhood was a struggle is to say the very least. What I did know from a young age was that I wanted more for my cousins, nieces, and daughters.

Growing up, I had the luxury of being around my mother, aunts, grandmothers, and a bonus mom. I thought being around all these women meant that I saw, heard, and knew all that I needed to know about being a woman. I thought that being uncomfortable in my skin was just part of "being a woman" and that the unwavering intrusive thoughts were just hormones and part of growing up. I learned about my body and sex from friends and first-hand experience, usually resulting in some form of pain or illness. When I was finally old enough to see a gynecologist, I felt I was too old to be asking silly questions about what my body was doing or how I was feeling, so I just tucked it away as I thought all women did. Who needs to know why I bleed as much and as long as I do or why it's so painful? Every woman bleeds and has cramps; I'm not weak and the world doesn't revolve around me so why make waves?

When I finally told my mother I was sexually active at a young age, I was met with disappointment and disdain. I thought I was being a responsible young adult and attempting to grow a closer relationship with my mom by being honest and open. There was never a conversation about how I felt, how IT felt, whether I had any questions, or about if I was okay. Nothing but silence and a stare. When she finally broke the silence, I was told I needed to be on birth control and that was the end of the sex talk for me. I felt ashamed and disgusted with myself. Maybe I had made a mistake having sex with my boyfriend of several years. Maybe I was being promiscuous and should have waited longer. Questions and self-doubt filled my brain, and to this day I still can't shake some of them out.

Years of on-and-off birth control, raging and swirling hormones, breast tumor scares, and pregnancy fears led me to stay silent. I never gabbed with girlfriends about periods or sex because I was scared I would say something that would be embarrassing. I didn't know everything and I didn't want to come across as stupid or inexperienced. It was easier to stay silent and figure it out on my own - or that's at least what I thought was easier.

As my life went on and I continued my education in the medical field, I thought that I would finally understand everything that I hadn't before. While I did learn many new and exciting things, not all of my questions were answered. Again, for fear of being made fun of and embarrassing myself, I kept what I didn't know to myself and trucked on with life. I soaked up all the information I could about the human body and how it worked. Learning how to bring a tiny human into this world with my hands and care for both mother and child simultaneously brought such joy into my life. Watching a child come into this world and the ambition it took for that mother to deliver amazed me and solidified that I wanted to be a mother one day.

As the years went on and I fell in love with my wonderful soulmate, we decided we wanted to be together forever. While my other half and I had not been together very long, we knew instantly we were meant to be. My soon-to-be husband was also a package deal- bonus kiddos included! I was euphoric; I got to be a stepmother to an adventurous, kind, and wild 9-year-old girl and a spunky, hilarious 6-year-old boy. Within nine months of being together, we married, and a month later I was pregnant. I was overjoyed and excited but I was absolutely terrified because I knew only what I had watched from family and friends on how to actually BE a mother.

During my pregnancy that summer, my stepdaughter had come from Texas to visit with us. We had an amazing summer full of adventures together. However, as the summer went on I noticed that her body was starting to have changes. Over the course of a few days, she had started to complain of lower abdominal pain, was very tired, and said that her chest was hurting her. I knew instantly that the time had come. But I'm not her mother and I did NOT want to step on anyone's toes or steal their moment with their daughter. I reached out and talked with her mom and verified it was ok to have a talk with her, and we did exactly that. We talked for hours about the changes her body was going through, what it would do in the future, and how to be smart and responsible. We had a conversation about sex and her power over her own body and choices. She sat in silence for most of the conversation as I covered basic anatomy and in-depth birth control choices. When the conversation ended and she pranced off to being a kid again, my brain swirled with doubt. Maybe it was too much for her. Maybe she didn't care or maybe she just didn't want to hear it from me. Was this the right time? Would this conversation suffice or would she need to know more? I just couldn't be sure, so I vowed to always keep the lines of communication open and be honest with her. I was sympathetic when she was having menstrual cramps and always made sure to get her what she needed. I would ask her questions all the time, probably too many questions too much of the time. However, it created a bond between us that allowed her to ask questions about her body when she had them. Then sex came up. I froze and sat in silence. What?! We're here already?! Deep breaths, don't panic. It dawned on me, this was it- this was my chance, my letter to my former self. How do I tell her everything about everything?

Embarking on that conversation with my stepdaughter was awkward by all accounts, but empowering. I was giving her knowledge that I never had and wish I had. We talked again for hours; this time was much more in-depth. She had so many good questions that were answered and wild urban myths we debunked. I felt I did her justice. While my stepdaughter was growing into her womanhood, I had another daughter who was 10 years behind her sister and I felt I was prepared for everything.

Life's funny in so many ways. One moment you feel prepared and ready to conquer the world and the next moment you can't get out of bed or manage a shower. After I had my daughter, I struggled with postpartum anxiety- which I had no clue was a "thing" until after I had my son a year later. I felt that everything needed to be done, but that I was the only one capable of doing it. The paranoia I had about leaving my kids to go anywhere other than work was insane and exhausting. Long story short, I was able to get the assistance I needed and realized my postpartum anxiety was actually just anxiety. Man, I'll tell you she is a beast to deal with even when you know what her name is. Anxiety, you are a liar and I don't believe you. Anxiety, you are the reason behind so many of my fears and hesitations and I will take no more. I began medication and felt immensely different - a whole new me.

Irony: a state of affairs or an event that seems deliberately contrary to what one expects and is often amusing as a result. This is perimenopause or menopause in general. Weeks of waking up with night sweats and hot flashes, dry and uncomfortable nether bits- I'd had enough and felt something was absolutely wrong and the doctor needed to figure it out. "Isn't anything before menopause, perimenopause?" I giggled. My doctor was not amused by my quip and informed me that perimenopause happens right before menopause-like a trailer to a movie you never wanted to see, let alone star in. No longer being the sheepish young lady of my past, I asked questions. A lot of questions. All the questions. This time I was told, "Well, it's different for everyone. Hot flashes or not. Hormone surges or none at all. Hair loss or hair growth. Just be prepared for anything." Well, then prepare I must.

I'm a mother and a 911 dispatcher. Being prepared is my life's work. If I'm not prepared and ready for all scenarios, then I am not myself. I waited and waited for some form of the grand finale of peri-menopause and the grand entrance of full-blown menopause. I gathered as many ice packs and fans as I could. Purchased myself all the vitamins and tweezers for every occasion I could think of. Yet as I waited, my hair thinned on my scalp but gave an abundance on my chin for my son to tell me I missed while plucking. While patiently looking forward to the arrival of this next stage of life, I felt like I needed chapstick for the lower lady lips. Cue hotter flashes and sweatier night sweats, sex drive exiting stage left, and nipple itching taking center stage with the cacophony of migraines and gas playing the chorus. This was it; here was her grand entrance that I'd been waiting for. Ironic, that perimenopause and menopause share all the symptoms and that my waiting period could be as long as 10 years before I'd be experiencing full-blown menopause. I was prepared to never be prepared, and for now, that was going to be all the preparation I could muster. Oh, and put on the shopping list: preparation H as well- that's not a fun one to be without when you need it most.

How was I going to wait 10 years- a decade- to want to have sex again? A decade before I felt like a woman in any sense once more. I knew my husband couldn't wait that long. Between his playful butt-grabbing and sexual innuendos- ugh, gross! Who wants sex right now?! I feel like a balding, sweaty, chaffed-up blob - who wants this right now? He did. He wanted me and I couldn't understand it. I finally broke one day and had enough. I yelled and screamed and cried and explained to him that I just didn't know how to be intimate anymore because there was no sex drive. I sat there, with tears rolling down my cheeks, and tried to explain that I wanted him forever, but that I couldn't find the desire to have sex. I explained everything that I had been going through for months and he sat there taking it all in. I thought, "This is it- the end of my marriage." He's going to call it quits and walk away, but could I blame him? Sex is such an important part of our lives and how we connect on a deeper level and here I was taking that away from him because my body decided to go full-on fritz mode in my thirties. He sat there in silence and just looked at me, searching for something I couldn't see. Then he calmly got down on his knees, put his head on my lap, and said the most profound thing I've ever heard in my life. Words I never knew I needed to hear until that exact moment and from the person I needed to hear them from the most.

"Baby, we will find a way through this together. You are not alone. I love you." Those words hit the dead center of my body and ignited something I hadn't realized I was missing. I did feel alone. I felt undesired and irritating, so I kept to myself. By keeping it all in, not sharing my experience, thoughts, and feelings I doused my own flame. It was at that moment, I threw gasoline on that fire. I had never felt so desired and attractive, but in my moment of raw honesty with my soul mate my tears turned to gasoline and fed that fire. I was able to let go of what I was preparing for and embrace what I wasn't prepared for: true love and yearning for my man to touch me. I needed love on a different level at this stage in my life. I needed to know and be confident in what I was giving and receiving in order to get the mood just right.

It wasn't the end as I had feared but yet another chapter of our story. While I have no idea what my future holds, I know I have two young girls behind me who need to learn what it means to me to be a woman. I have years of knowledge and experience to bestow upon them and their brothers, who may not be as willing to learn about womanhood but will nonetheless. Being a woman and the voyage through any stage of womanhood can be a struggle, but we are never alone. Ever.

# WISDOM OF WOMANHOOD

## By Prudence Todd

Many would say wisdom comes from the lived experience, living out the knowledge we have acquired in life, and learning from it. This may be true in many ways, after all, how can one truly understand an experience until they've lived through it? In recent years, however, I have noticed in and through my work with women that we can access an intuitive wisdom that rests within our bodies from a very young age. I've seen this in my clients and also with my daughter who is twenty-one and so very deeply wise. I believe this is because of my willingness and ability to access my own body's wisdom and teach her to do the same.

Recently I asked a few different communities of women what Womanhood Wisdom meant for them. Some of the answers I received were:

*"Gaining wisdom through the transitions and initiations of Womanhood – I am constantly in deep honor for those who have walked before me."* —Ellie

*"Lineages of wisdom that are awakened in this lifetime through our initiation and experiences, and fed by the creative life force within the womb."* —Lucy

*"The divine, sexual, creative, feminine, fertile energy. Moon cycles. Trusting in the cycles of life and all its cycles. It makes me feel powerful."* —Anonymous

I love these responses so much and as I read through all that women shared I wondered, "Do we as women think of Womanhood Wisdom as a beautiful concept to look upon (a romantic idea), or do we really feel we have access to it within our own life, heart, and body?" I invite you to sit with this question, Sweet Woman. I wonder what your answer is. If you feel a sense of disconnect, numbness, or unfamiliarity, I am here to encourage you to access the Wisdom of Womanhood no matter what age you are, what you've been through, what you're longing for, or how long you've been feeling this way. You have wisdom within you. And you CAN access it.

## Collective Wisdom

Eighteen months ago, I was moved to gather women together from different generations and thus the community *Reconnecting Maidens, Mummas, and Grandmammas* was born. My hope was for women to share wisdom, love, and connection across different phases of life. This community of women has gathered and grown over the past 12 months and shared so much. Women have felt seen, heard, and held through simply sharing wisdom, time together, and heart connections. When I birthed this gathering, I noticed a nudge within me to really step up and lead women with love. I felt resistance straight away with the thought "Oh but you're not wise enough to lead women!" I believed this to be true for some time until I felt the nudge again and again.

During this time I was also seeing women in my clinic and online who felt heartbroken, disconnected, invalidated, unsure, guilty, and ashamed due to their experiences as a woman in this world. In our time together I watched these women feel safe enough to become vulnerable, soft enough to be held, and surrender enough to be led towards their inner wisdom. They would leave after their session feeling much lighter, more confident, open-hearted, validated, and deeply connected. I began to trust my own inner knowing to hold and lead women home in their bodies, to know truth and wisdom for themselves.

## My Journey

I grew up in a Christian home believing that I was loved and accepted if I was living life a certain way. Although I learned about God and his love and knew this in my heart, I also learned about what God didn't like and what choices were not ok. When I went through my teenage years – the duality of my life was soul-crushing. I wanted one thing – to be peaceful according to what I was taught God wanted of me. But I also wanted life experience – and the two warred within me. So, I tried to live with both and consequently experienced shame and guilt most days.

When I became a mother all of this that I had carried in my heart came to a head. I was going to be the most graceful, patient Mumma but consequently, I became a SUPER depressed Mumma with fierce expectations of myself to always be peaceful, calm, and kind; to look a certain way, to have obedient children, and so on. I placed huge pressure on myself to perform, have a peaceful home, and please my parents, even as an adult. This pressure would build up and explode at my children, my husband, and myself as rage. I had zero compassion, awareness, or love for the little girl within who was now a Mumma, and didn't know how to heal herself.

My journey with depression came to a pivotal point when my husband left our home due to the incessant fighting in front of our children. He was broken, I was broken, and we just couldn't do it anymore. We no longer wanted to hide, pretending everything was ok, when behind closed doors our relationship was heart-wrenchingly broken. I started my own healing journey; as did he after many years of trying to support me and my depression.

During my healing, I came across a few words that said, *"I cannot be a responsible parent if I'm still trying to be an obedient daughter."* WOW - this hit me so deeply. Like a fist to my belly. I was trying so hard to 'get it right' to be the 'perfect mumma' that I had lost sight of what I needed for myself to be who I wanted to be in the world. How could I truly love myself, my partner, and my children, if subconsciously all I knew was to be obedient to something or someone else?

After 12 months of separation, counseling, fierce listening, and healing, my husband and I reunited. We have been together now for twenty-five years and to this day I know the JOY of my relationship is consequently connected to the JOY of my WOMANHOOD. How well I communicate with myself and how I draw on my own wisdom. Developing a deep love connection with myself has healed so much in the relationships around me.

As a child, I learned to trust in a God greater than myself, but now I have also learned to trust in the inner knowing within me. My journey of healing the oppression in my heart and body is foundational in the way I guide other women. If we cannot connect to the woman who is longing to be seen, how can we ever truly heal?

What will it take for you, Sweet Woman, to see her?

## Trust

How do we learn to trust? When I was young, I was taught the concept of trust, but it wasn't until I was an adult and experienced the sudden loss of my brother that I really learned to trust. I remember being so racked with the pain of grief for so long that my body started to experience debilitating anxiety for the first time. Constantly wondering what might go wrong next was no way to live. I began to take my concerns into quietness. To ask the deeper questions of life in stillness and to be quiet and listen. All the things I had been taught started to fall away and for the first time in my life, I felt a deep ease in not having to know the answers. This opened me up to being guided in the moment, and even having my children guide the way and allowing myself to release the weight of "needing to know it all" as a parent. I also discovered I had lost my faith in life due to life's traumas and deep grief. I learned how to reconnect to life. I built trust in her again so I could meet her with joy and an open heart, instead of fear and mistrust.

I am so deeply grateful for the experiences I have been through that caused me to pull apart and rebuild myself as a woman. Without them I wouldn't be who I am today nor would I be able to guide women the way I do.

## Where Do We Source Wisdom Within Us?

Generally, we think of wisdom as coming from the heart and mind; for women, however, I have witnessed their deepest source of wisdom is from the womb. Why would we glean wisdom from our womb? If we think about it, we were created here, lived here, cycle, and menstruate from here, and for many of us, we carry life within us here. So, there's a lot of cellular memory and consciousness resting, waiting for us to access it. I do believe that the more connected we are to our cycles, not just menstruation but all of our cycle and how we relate to our body, plays a part in how we connect to our deeper, womanhood wisdom. If we were shamed, caused to feel like we needed to hide our bleed, led to believe we were dirty, felt like an inconvenience, or that our periods just didn't matter and perhaps lived without having a cycle or bleed (an option many women take since the introduction of the pill), we miss the deeper connection to our womanhood and what she is trying to teach us. I believe really understanding our cycles is the first step to our Womanhood wisdom. Our connection with our cycles impacts how we relate to birth and also how we relate to ourselves as women after we birth our babies. Particularly, if we had a challenging birth (see chapter 12). These experiences of birth and how we see ourselves as mothers and women also impact our experience of menopause. Many women I work with going through menopause discover they have been unaware of how their body functions and carry veils of shame and guilt about many aspects of their lives. As we unveil these and step into a true love connection with ourselves, women start to experience freedom and joy in life itself. This, Sweet Woman, is why I don't believe it simply takes time and life experience to be wise. I believe we are born with body wisdom and it grows with us as we journey through life, but sadly we don't grow up being shown how to access it.

## So How Do We Access the Wisdom of Womanhood?

Let's do a little exercise together.

Take five minutes. Sit or lie in a comfortable position and be still. Focus on your breath and as you breathe in draw it down into your belly. Softly exhale. As you take your next breath, let your belly relax and allow your breath to flow down and nourish your womb (even if you don't have one anymore, energetically she is still there and you can connect with her). Take a moment to acknowledge your body, your womb, and all she has been through. All she has created and carried. All she has released. Be still and speak the words to her: " I love you and I am so deeply thankful." Notice how your body feels.

Such a simple exercise and yet so much connection can be felt by simply tuning in with loving intent. You can connect this way to all your organs within the pelvic space and marvelously they will all have different messages for you, depending on what your body needs. Our body is so deeply wise!

I touched on earlier the reality that we all want to be womanly wise, but not all of us feel it in our bodies. What would it mean to you to feel womanly wise?

Some of the attributes I have come to know in my body as womanly wisdom that I would love to honor here are:

- tender love
- unbiased judgment
- compassion
- the practice and experimentation of self-knowledge
- developing a deep reverence for life

- the deep healing and transmutation of our trauma

I love to witness these attributes develop in women as they learn to love themselves for all they've been through. One of my clients who had been seeing me for pelvic wellness recently shared, "My daughter asked me, Mum, what have you been doing? Something has changed and it is beautiful!" What's so very special about this is not only a woman experiencing such lightness and joy through connecting within, but her daughter witnessing this enough to ask for herself!

This is the ultimate goal for me through knowing Womanhood Wisdom - to be able to pass what we come to know to our daughters and our sons so they can also share with the world. I know my sons, though they may cringe and laugh at the many things I share, are absorbing many snippets of info along the way that will help them understand women in their lives. When women are more deeply seen, heard, and understood, how wonderful is that?! I believe the true balance and healing of our relationships in this world comes from the deeper balancing and healing of ourselves. Learning to have compassion for others comes from having compassion for ourselves.

A few weeks ago I was sitting, witnessing a beautiful woman resting deep into laboring with her first child. At times she called on me to aid her in what she needed but for the most part, it was simply my presence that was needed to witness her go through the experience. This is how the journey of Womanhood is really. At some point, we are called from the everyday into a deep surrender - mostly through life experiences, physical symptoms, illness, or the birth or death of a loved one. Just being seen by another in all we are going through can be so healing and truly seeing another begins with truly seeing ourselves.

What wisdom is resting within you calling to be seen, Sweet Woman? Do you need support to guide you? Reach out if you do. It's never too late to begin learning how to deeply listen and connect to our inner wisdom and the wisdom of those who've walked before and beside us. If this has stirred something within you and you feel moved to connect with me you can find me on Instagram as YOUR WOMANHOOD or go to my linktree link below.

Sending you so much love and light. Thank you for sharing all I have expressed here. Keep listening in Dear One, as one person said "Wisdom is there for all who sit quiet enough to listen for it."

linktr.ee/prudencetodd
www.instagram.com/yourwomanhood/

# EMBRACING THE EMPOWERED WOMAN

As we come to the end of this transformative journey through *Womanhood*, I am filled with a profound sense of gratitude for the shared experiences, candid conversations, and unwavering support that have defined our exploration of womanhood.

In the stories woven together within these pages, we have discovered the strength of vulnerability and the beauty of authenticity. Each chapter has offered a glimpse into the lives of remarkable women, each one navigating their unique paths with courage, resilience, and determination.

Throughout this journey, we have challenged societal norms, shattered the silence surrounding taboo topics, and uplifted the voices of those who have often been marginalized. We have celebrated the richness of diversity and embraced the power of inclusivity, acknowledging that womanhood is not confined to one mold, but encompasses a multitude of experiences, identities, and narratives.

Yet, the conversations aren't over. In fact, they are just beginning.

The power of authentic conversations has been our guiding light, illuminating the shadows of shame and empowering us to reclaim our stories. By sharing our triumphs and struggles, we have forged a powerful bond—a sisterhood that transcends borders and bridges gaps.

To every reader who has journeyed with us, we extend our heartfelt appreciation. It is through your willingness to engage in these vital dialogues that we can collectively redefine womanhood and create a safer, more compassionate world for all women.

As we part ways, we encourage you to carry forward the spirit of this book into your own lives. Share your stories, support one another, and create spaces where authenticity can flourish. Remember that your voice matters, and by speaking your truth, you empower others to do the same.

Together, we are an unstoppable force, capable of breaking down barriers, challenging injustices, and shaping a brighter future for generations to come.

The journey of womanhood is not linear; it is a tapestry of intertwining threads, each one contributing to the beauty of the whole. Embrace your unique thread, celebrate your resilience, and cherish the connections you make along the way.

Thank you for joining us on this transformative voyage. May the conversations ignited within these pages continue to ripple outward, sparking change and empowerment in the hearts of all who encounter them.

With love, solidarity, and hope,
Your Sisters in Womanhood

# RESOURCES

*Your path to empowerment is personal and unique. We encourage you to research and utilize external resources with discernment. While we've made every effort to provide helpful information, we cannot guarantee the accuracy, completeness, or suitability of external sources. Please exercise due diligence.*

## SELF-LOVE, IDENTITY, AND EXPRESSION

The Body Positive - www.thebodypositive.org

- Non-profit organization dedicated to promoting body acceptance and self-love. They offer educational programs and workshops that empower individuals to redefine beauty and embrace body positivity.

National Eating Disorders Association (NEDA) - www.nationaleatingdisorders.org

- Leading non-profit organization dedicated to supporting individuals and families affected by eating disorders.

Majik Mentality - heal.me/bewise

- Holistic healing business dedicated to the health and well-being of women transitioning into motherhood. Clients are offered a variety of healing modalities to foster better self-care and self-love practices to combat anxiety, depression, or other stress-related ailments.

## SEXUALITY

Pure Romance - www.pureromance.com/krystalcasey

- Offers a wide range of products and resources to promote sexual health, well-being, and empowerment for women.

**Girl Boner Radio** - augustmclaughlin.com/podcast/

- A spicy blend of personal stories, in-depth reporting, and inspiration hosted by health and sexuality writer August McLaughlin.

## RELATIONSHIPS

**LOVER: Ultimate Intimacy App** - loverapp.krystalcasey.com

- App dedicated to fostering intimacy and connection between partners.

**The Adventure Challenge** - tac.krystalcasey.com

- Book of scratch-off challenges where you'll uncover mystery activities that revitalize your relationships and create lasting memories with your loved one.

## SELF ADVOCACY

**BADASS MILF Bootcamp** - jenslifecoaching.com

- 4 week course to unlock your inner power and become the independent, confident woman of your dreams.

**Service Women's Action Network** (SWAN) - www.servicewomen.org

- Non-profit organization that provides support, resources, and legal assistance to women who have experienced misogyny, discrimination, or sexual assault during their military service.

**RAINN** - www.rainn.org

- Provides support for survivors of sexual violence and advocacy to prevent sexual assault.

# MOTHERHOOD

**Your Womanhood** - www.facebook.com/groups/healafterbirthtrauma/

- A supportive Facebook group offering healing and support for mothers who have experienced birth trauma.

**The Mama Sutra** - www.themamasutra.com

- Platform dedicated to providing valuable resources and support for parents to navigate conversations about sex.

**Dougy** - www.dougy.org

- Provides resources and support for parents navigating grief after losing a child.

**All-Options** - www.all-options.org/

- Offers a hotline providing free, confidential support for all pregnancy options, including abortion, adoption, and parenting.

# LIFE'S TRANSITIONS

**From Stuck to Unstoppable: Rising From the Ashes** - www.momstransform.com

- A virtual course empowering moms to redesign their lives after overcoming trauma or tragedy.

**Hope for Widows** - www.hopeforwidows.org/blog/

- Non-profit offering support, resources, and stories for widows navigating grief and healing.

**Navigating Menopause and Reclaiming Vitality** - www.womenshealth.gov/menopause

- Provides information and resources on menopause and reclaiming well-being.

# SPREAD YOUR WINGS!
# #FLIGHTOFTHEPHOENIXCOLLECTIVE

### *Rising From the Ashes*
### With Flight of the Phoenix:
### A Women's Empowerment Collective

Congratulations on successfully embarking on the transformative journey that is *Womanhood: Identity to Intimacy and Everything in Between.* We trust that this exploration of the intricate tapestry of womanhood has awakened a vibrant fire within you—an inner strength nurtured by passion, desire, and sensuality. With this newfound inspiration, you're now poised to embrace the world with renewed vigor.

Meet Krystal Casey, a remarkable woman and a devoted mother of five. She is a beacon of empowerment, driven by an unrelenting passion to help women rediscover their purpose, voice, and inner fire. Krystal's vision has given birth to *Flight of the Phoenix: A Women's Empowerment Collective,* an oasis of empowerment for women from all walks of life.

## Discover Flight of the Phoenix:
## A Women's Empowerment Collective

At Flight of the Phoenix, we are more than a collective; we are a haven. Our guiding principle is community-driven empowerment where we provide steadfast support, invaluable resources, and expert guidance to navigate the most challenging chapters of life. Our unwavering commitment is to nurture and empower women to rise above these challenges, helping them emerge as powerful and resilient individuals.

Your journey doesn't end with the last page of this book—it's merely the beginning. We warmly invite you to continue your voyage of self-discovery, resilience, and empowerment. Here at Flight of the Phoenix, we are here for you, ready to guide and support you as you soar to new heights.

# Ready To Reignite Your Passion
# And Rediscover Your Voice?

If you're ready to elevate your personal growth to the next level, consider enrolling in our transformative course, *From Stuck to Unstoppable.* Tailored for women from all walks of life, this course equips you with the tools, guidance, and unwavering support needed to embrace your unstoppable self, even when confronted with life's challenges. Sign up at momstransform.com.

## Connect with Us

Stay abreast of our latest content, upcoming events, and engaging discussions. Become a part of our online community, check out our other books, and follow us on social media.

**Find Your Voice, Ignite Your Fire**: Unlock the door to meaningful conversations and deep explorations of womanhood. *The Ladies Lounge* is your exclusive, safe haven, where women aged 18 and up gather to discuss taboo topics and empower one another. You're invited to join us at www.facebook.com/groups/flightofthephoenixladieslounge/.

**Have You Read Our Other Empowering Collection?** If you haven't yet explored the stories within *Shattering the Stigma of Single Motherhood,* we encourage you to delve into this inspiring journey. This powerful book is filled with incredible narratives and life-changing insights that will touch your heart and mind.
Find it at Barnes and Noble, Amazon, or your favorite book retailers.

Stay tuned for upcoming books that will continue
to empower and inspire!

**Ready To Dive Even Deeper?** Consider hiring <u>Krystal Casey</u> as a
speaker to inspire your audience or event coordinator for your next
empowering event.

For more information about the course, hiring Krystal as a speaker or
event planner, or any of our empowering resources, please email her
at <u>contact@flightofthephoenixcollective.com</u>. At Flight of the
Phoenix, we're here to support your journey to greatness and can't
wait to watch you soar!